RIVER & STREAMS IN THE DESERT

The Forty Forties of Scripture—A Forty-Day Repentance Devotional

PASTOR JEFFREY DALY

WESTBOW
PRESS®
A DIVISION OF THOMAS NELSON
& ZONDERVAN

WestBow Press books may be ordered through booksellers or by contacting:

WestBow Press
A Division of Thomas Nelson & Zondervan
1663 Liberty Drive
Bloomington, IN 47403
www.westbowpress.com
1 (866) 928-1240

ISBN: 978-1-9736-6185-6 (sc)
ISBN: 978-1-9736-6186-3 (hc)
ISBN: 978-1-9736-6187-0 (e)

Library of Congress Control Number: 2019906876

Print information available on the last page.

WestBow Press rev. date: 06/29/2019

Contents

River & Streams in the Desert

The Forty Forties of Scripture
~ A Forty Day Repentance Devotional

There is a river whose streams make glad the city of God,
The holy dwelling places of the Most High.
God is in the midst of her, she will not be moved;
God will help her when morning dawns.
~ Psalm 46: 4-5 (NASB)

The wilderness and the wasteland shall be glad for them,
And the desert shall rejoice and blossom as the rose; It
shall blossom abundantly and rejoice, Even with joy and
singing. The glory of Lebanon shall be given to it, The
excellence of Carmel and Sharon. They shall see the glory
of the LORD, The excellency of our God. Strengthen
the weak hands, And make firm the feeble knees. Say to
those who are fearful-hearted, "Be strong, do not fear!
Behold your God will come with vengeance, With the
recompense of God; He will come and save you.' Then
the eyes of the blind shall be opened, And the ears of the
deaf shall be unstopped. Then the lame shall leap like a
deer, And the tongue of the dumb sing. For waters shall
burst forth in the wilderness, And streams in the desert.
~ Isaiah 35: 1-6(NKJV)

This Book is Dedicated to:
Yeshua

You are the Mighty God, the Prince of Peace, The Word made Flesh, The Lord of Glory, The Resurrection and the Life, the Creator of all things, our Lord and Savior, God of the whole Earth, God made manifest, The God of Abraham, Isaac and Jacob, the Highest, The Lord of Hosts, Mighty in Battle, our Righteousness, the One Who is, Who was and Who is to come, the Upholder of Everything, the Everlasting God, The Beginning, the End, The First and the Last, The Messenger of the Covenant, The Messiah, The Deliverer, The Lamb that was slain, The Bridegroom, the Good Shepherd, The Way, The Door, The Truth, The Bishop of our souls, The Branch, The Vine, The Tree of Life, The Bread of Life, The Rose of Sharon, the Lily of the Valley, The Light, The Bright and Morning Star, The Day-Spring from on High, a Refuge from the Storm, The Horn of our Salvation, The Rock of Ages, Our Fortress, Our Strength, Our Refuge, Our Redeemer, The Builder, The Foundation, The Chief Corner-Stone, Our Ransom, Our Great High Priest, Our Mediator, Our Intercessor, Our Advocate, Faithful and True, a Faithful Witness, The Holy and Just One, The Head of the Church, man and all principalities and powers, The Author and Finisher of our Faith, The Lion of the Tribe of Judah, our Shield, Lord of both the dead and the living, Lord of the Sabbath, Lord of Peace, The Glory of Thy people Israel, The Righteous Judge who shall reign forever and ever, King of the Jews, King of the Saints, King of all the nations, King over all the Earth, King of Righteousness, King of Peace, King of Glory, King crowned with many crowns, a King that reigns forever, Fairer than the children of men, A Brother born for adversity, A Friend that stays closer than a brother, A Friend that loves at all times, Your Countenance is as the Sun, You are altogether Lovely, You were Obedient, Meek, Lowly, Guileless, Tempted, Oppressed, Despised, Rejected, Betrayed, Condemned, Reviled, Scourged, Mocked, Wounded, Bruised, Stricken, Smitten, Crucified, Forsaken, You are

Merciful, Faithful, Holy, Undefiled, Separate, Perfect, Glorious, Mighty, Justified, Exalted, Risen and Glorified. You are my Portion, my Maker, my Husband, my Well-Beloved, my Savior, my Hope, my Brother, my Helper, my Physician, my Healer, my Refiner, my Purifier, my Lord, my Master, my Example, my Teacher, my Shepherd, my Keeper, my Feeder, my Leader, my Restorer, my Resting-place, my Meat, my Drink, my Peace, my Wisdom, my Righteousness, my Sanctification, my Redemption, Emmanuel, God with us, The Lord of lords, King of kings, the Name above all names.

My All in All

There are many more things that You are. If all of them were written down, I suppose that not even the world itself would have space for the books that would be written.
(John 21:25 Berean Study Bible)

Onward

It is typically in this section of most books that you will find a "Foreword" and/or a "Preface." However, I have deliberately titled this page as the "Onward" instead. Too often we think that we *precede* God's wondrous work of intervention when, in fact, we simply have the honor of responding to His casting call. Now here is where many people will get into the theological debate which is about the equivalency of *"What came first the Chicken or the Egg?"* I will not do that here. Did John the Baptist, the greatest Repentance preacher born of woman, precede Jesus Christ? In a manner of speaking one may say "yes." However, did he really precede the One Who was, Who Is and Who always will be?

In doing the research for this book, I have learned (and continue to learn) many things. A Foreword is typically written by someone other than the Author in order to offer a witness to his credibility and why people should read the book. A Preface is written by the Author himself to explain how his book came into being. Pondering these definitions, it became obvious that neither was really appropriate here.

HE is the One who justifies our Work. If He prompted this work, it will be deemed worthy. If not, it will be burned up as straw in the end. HE is the Author and Finisher of our faith and, after centuries of heated theological debate, we still can't fully explain where this process begins and ends. God's Holy Word goes before us, the Fore-"word," if you will. Jesus is the Pre-"face" to illuminate this faith process of becoming.

Does God know who will and who will not ultimately come into agreement with Him? Does He know who will be favored by grace? Sure. He knows everything. That is not the question. As Shakespeare succinctly stated, *"To be or not to be, that is the question."* That *is* the question! That is the question we need to each ask ourselves. *Will we be faithful* so that we may continue to "be" with Christ throughout eternity?

This book is submitted for your review upon this belief that we must continue to remain faithful in reliance upon the Faithful One. If He authors the work of Repentance, He will most certainly finish it as well. He will judge those of us who participate in His Grand Epic Drama. Suffice it to say, as the Script-Writer, His Ways are higher than our ways and His Thoughts are higher than our thoughts. We only "see through a glass darkly."

It is my prayer that this Devotional helps your faith increase so that you may affirmatively answer His call with: "I am the Lord's servant. May it happen to me according to Your Word."

Jesus Himself asks us this question:

> *"Nevertheless, when the Son of Man comes, will He find faith on earth?"*   (Luke 18:8 Berean Study Bible)

Will He?

Introduction ~ A Way in the Wilderness

The number 40 in the Bible is quite possibly one of the most significantly repeated numbers in scripture. In preparing the research for this Devotional, we came upon these "forty forties" for you to ponder.

Day #1: 40 days of rain

And the rain was upon the earth <u>forty days</u> and forty nights.
~ Genesis 7:12 (NKJV)

Day #2: 40 nights of rain

And the rain was upon the earth forty days and <u>forty nights</u>.
~ Genesis 7:12 (NKJV)

Day #3: 40 righteous in Sodom and God would not have destroyed it

Once again Abraham spoke to the LORD, "Suppose <u>forty</u> are found there?" He answered, "On account of the <u>forty</u>, I will not do it." ~ Genesis 18:29 (Berean Study Bible)

Day #4: 40 years old when Isaac took Rebekah as his wife

And Isaac was <u>forty years old</u> when he took Rebekah to wife
~ Genesis 25:20 (KJV)

Day #5: 40 years old when Esau took a wife

When Esau was <u>forty years old</u>, he took as his wives Judith daughter of Beeri the Hittite and Basemath daughter of Elon the Hittite. ~ Genesis 26:34 (Berean Study Bible)

Day # 6: 40 days Israel embalmed in Egypt before buried in Canaan

And Joseph directed the physicians in his service to embalm his father Israel. So they embalmed him, taking the <u>forty days</u> required to complete the embalming.

~ Genesis 50:2-3(a) (Berean Study Bible)

Day #7: 40 years Moses lived in Egypt before leading Israel

So Moses was educated in all the wisdom of the Egyptians and was powerful in speech and action. When Moses was <u>forty years old</u>, he decided to visit his brothers, the sons of Israel.

~ Acts 7:22-23 (Berean Study Bible)

Day #8: 40 more years Moses in wilderness before leading Israel

After <u>forty years</u> had passed, an angel appeared to Moses in the flames of a burning bush in the desert near Mount Sinai.

~ Acts 7:30 (NIV)

Day #9: 40 years that the children of Israel ate manna

The Israelites ate manna <u>forty years</u>, until they came to a land where they could settle; they ate manna until they reached the border of Canaan.   ~ Exodus 16:35 (NIV)

Day #10: 40 years the Israelites wandered in the wilderness

And your children shall wander in the wilderness forty years, and bear your whoredoms, until your carcasses be wasted in the wilderness.   ~Numbers 14:33 (KJV)

Day #11: 40 years the garments of children of Israel did not wear out

Your clothing did not wear out and your feet did not swell during these <u>forty years</u>.

~ Deuteronomy 8:4 (Berean Study Bible)

Day #12: 40 days Moses spent getting the Law Tablets the 1ˢᵗ time

Moses entered the cloud as he went up on the mountain, and he remained on the mountain <u>forty days</u> and <u>forty nights</u>.

~ Exodus 24:18

Day #13: 40 days Moses spent getting the Law Tablets the 2ⁿᵈ time

I stayed on the mountain <u>forty days</u> and <u>forty nights</u>, like the first time, and that time the LORD again listened to me and agreed not to destroy you.

~ Deuteronomy 10:10 (Berean Study Bible)

Day #14: 40 years age when Caleb spied out the Promised Land

I was <u>forty years old</u> when Moses the servant of the LORD sent me from Kadesh-barnea to spy out the land, and I brought back to him an honest report.

~ Joshua 14:7 (Berean Study Bible)

Day #15: 40 days Joshua & Caleb went to spy the Promised Land

And they returned from searching of the land after <u>forty days</u>.

~ Numbers 13:25 (KJV)

Day 16: 40 chapters in the Book of Exodus

For the cloud of the LORD was on the tabernacle by day, and fire was in it by night, in the sight of all the house of Israel throughout all their journeys. ~ Exodus <u>40</u>:38 (ESV)

Day 17: 40 years of peace under Judge Othniel ruling Israelites

So the land had rest for <u>forty years</u>, until Othniel son of Kenaz died. ~ Judges 3:11 (Berean Study Bible)

Day 18: 40 years rest after Deborah inspired Israel to Victory

So may all your enemies perish, O LORD, But may those who love You shine like the sun at its brightest. And the land had rest for forty years. ~ Judges 5:31 (Berean Study Bible)

Day 19: 40 years served by Judge Barak with Israelites

And the princes of Issachar were with Deborah; even Issachar, and also Barak: he was sent on foot into the valley. And the land had rest for forty years. ~ Judges 5:15 & 31(b) (KJV)

Day 20: 40 years of peace after Gideon's conquest

So the land had rest for forty years in the days of Gideon. ~ Judges 8:28(b) (Berean Study Bible)

Day 21: 40 days the Philistine Goliath taunted Israel

And the Philistine drew near morning and evening, and presented himself forty days. ~ 1 Samuel 17:16 (KJV)

Day 22: 40 years of bondage to the Philistines before Samson born

And the children of Israel did evil again in the sight of the Lord; and the Lord delivered them into the hand of the Philistines forty years. ~ Judges 13:1 (KJV)

Day 23: 40 years Eli was a judge before the glory departed from Israel (Ichabod)

Eli had judged Israel forty years. ~ 1 Samuel 4:18(b) (Berean Study Bible)

Day 24: 40 stripes = the maximum punishment for the wicked man

*He may receive no more than <u>forty lashes</u>, lest your brother be
beaten any more than that and be degraded in your sight.*
~ Deuteronomy 25:3 (Berean Study Bible)

Day #25: 40 days/nights Elijah's strength
lasted after eat/drink from angels

*So he got up and ate and drank. And strengthened by that food,
he walked <u>forty days</u> and <u>forty nights</u> until he reached Horeb,
the mountain of God.* ~ 1 Kings 19:8 (Bercan Study Bible)

Day #26: 40 camels sent to Elisha to enquire if king would recover

*So Hazael went to meet Elisha, taking with him a gift of <u>forty
camel-loads</u> of every good thing from Damascus.*
~2 Kings 8:9(a) (Berean Study Bible)

Day #27: 40 years of King Jehoash's reign

*Joash was seven years old when he became king, and he reigned
in Jerusalem <u>forty years</u>.* ~ 2 Chronicles 24:1(a) (NIV)

Day #28: 40 "by the space of" God gave Israel King Saul

*And afterward they desired a king: and God gave unto them
Saul the son of Cis, a man of the tribe of Benjamin, by the space
of <u>forty years</u>.* ~ Acts 13:21 (KJV)

Day #29: 40 years David reigned over Israel

*The length of David's reign over Israel was <u>forty years</u>—seven
years in Hebron and thirty-three years in Jerusalem.*
~ 1 Kings 2:11 (Berean Study Bible)

Day #30: 40 years Solomon reigned over Israel

Solomon reigned in Jerusalem over all Israel <u>forty years</u>.
~ 2 Chronicles 9:30 (NIV)

Day #31: 40 sockets of silver to build the Temple

And for the other side of the tabernacle, which is toward the north corner, he made twenty boards, And their <u>forty sockets of silver</u>; two sockets under one board, and two sockets under another board. ~ Exodus 36: 25-26 (KJV)

Day #32: 40 days Nineveh had to repent and be overturned

On the first day of his walk, Jonah set out into the city and proclaimed, <u>"Forty more days</u> and Nineveh will be overturned!"
~ Jonah 3:4 (Berean Study Bible)

Day #33: 40 days Ezekiel laid on right side to symbolize Judah's sins

When you have completed these days, lie down again, but on your right side, and bear the iniquity of the house of Judah. I have assigned to you <u>40 days</u>, a day for each year.
~ Ezekiel 4:6 (Berean Study Bible)

Day #34: 40 days and nights Jesus fasted in the wilderness

And having fasted <u>forty days and forty nights</u>, afterward He was hungry. ~ Matthew 4:2 (Berean Literal Bible)

Day #35: 40 days Jesus appeared to followers after His resurrection

After His suffering, He presented Himself to them with many convincing proofs that He was alive. He appeared to them over a span of <u>forty days</u> and spoke about the kingdom of God.
~ Acts 1:3 (Berean Study Bible)

Day #36: 40 symbolic years in a biblical generation

And the Lord's anger was kindled against Israel, and He made them wander in the wilderness <u>forty years, until all the generation</u> that had done evil in the sight of the Lord was consumed. ~ Numbers 32:13 (KJV)

Day #37: 40 years after Crucifixion the Destruction of the Temple

And answering, He said to them, "Do you not see all these things? Truly I say to you, no not even a stone shall be left here upon a stone, which will not be thrown down." ~ Matthew 24:2 (Berean Literal Bible) (<u>event occurred 40 years later</u>)

Day #38: 40 years of age or over the man healed by Peter and John

For the man was <u>over forty years old</u> on whom this miracle of healing had been performed. ~ Acts 4:22 (NKJV)

Day #39: 40 and more men vowed not to eat/drink until Paul killed

<u>*More than forty of them*</u> *were involved in this plot.* ~ Acts 23:12-13 (Berean Study Bible)

Day #40: 40 stripes "save one" was the whipping Paul endured

Five times Of the Jews five times received I <u>forty stripes</u> save one. ~ 2 Corinthians 11:24 (KJV)

Please enjoy reading our "Forty Forties" repentance devotionals as we follow along this scriptural pathway. Each day will also offer a short repentance prayer as a simple outline for you to participate in your own personal repentance time.

Our hope is to encourage you to search the scriptures in order to find new insights into God's gift of repentance. We pray that, along with the Holy Spirit's guidance, you will become zealous to repent from old sin patterns and be inspired to be a daily witness to others as you joyfully prepare as His Bride.

Join us as we walk together through the "forty forties" of scripture.

PRAYER:

O Lord, according to Your Word, let us enter into Your gates with Thanksgiving and into Your courts with praise. Most High God, Master and Creator of the Universe, we humbly bow before You and worship You, each of us with all of our heart, soul and mind. As Jesus instructed us, we start this prayer with praise and a sense of thankfulness—deeply grateful that You DO, indeed, hear the prayers of Your children. You tell us that the prayer of a righteous man has great power to prevail. (James 5:16 Berean Study Bible)

We acknowledge the incredible right and privilege You have given us to walk directly into the Presence of the most Powerful and Effective might in the Universe and **BOLDLY** ask for assistance. The devils tremble at this privilege which You have afforded us through the Blood of Jesus Christ. Help us to fully take hold of the extent of this opportunity. Forgive us for the time when we have not utilized this right effectively through lack of Faith.

Lord Most High, we are in dire need of Your assistance. There are forces afoot that would attempt to destroy all of Your Creation—forces that seek to steal, kill and destroy Your Church. You said that we would have Life and have it more abundantly. You said the gates of Hell would not prevail against Your Church. Thus, for YOUR sake, O God, and based on the unfailing promises of Your Holy Word, do not let the forces of evil and darkness prevail. We ask that Righteousness, Peace and Joy would abound in order that Your Name would be honored and glorified. We believe that both Israel and other "bridal nations" were founded expressly on Your Principles in their Law and Constitutions. These nation states were formed for Your Glory and providentially placed under Your Covenantal Contract to be shining cities upon a hill whose Beacon Light was to guide freedom-loving people and other nations globally to Jesus Christ.

We acknowledge our failure in the Body of Christ to properly keep our side of the Covenant. We have NOT lived as we should. We have NOT obeyed all of Your commands. We have NOT placed You first in our lives. We confess that our nations are currently on a dangerous pathway towards the idolatry of Human Secularism, which seeks to remove You from every aspect of our daily public lives and set up ourselves as gods instead. In doing so, we have not only failed to follow in Christ's footsteps to help "set the captives free," but, instead, we ourselves have become captives to an un-Godly philosophy that, if not repented of, will ultimately destroy our countries.

O God, we sincerely REPENT of our personal and national sins. We REPENT of the sins of omission as well as commission. These sins include idolatry, murder, anger, stubbornness, dishonesty, corruption, greed, sloth, lust, envy, compromise, fear, gluttony, gossip, hypocrisy, impurity, ingratitude, profanity, stealing, unforgiveness, untruthfulness, worldliness, worry and, the ultimate sin, Pride. We take no solace in the fact that some of us may not have personally embraced sins such as abortion, marriage redefinition or false religions BUT, by apathy or indifference, we have allowed this evil to flourish. We have not followed Your Biblical mandate to submit to You, to obey Your Holy commandments and resist Satan nor have we had a zeal to REPENT which invites You to commune with us, enabling us to become overcomers who will sit with You on Your Throne (Revelation 3:19-21).

Instead of embracing righteousness we, both individually and in our families and in our nations, have performed evil acts. We have fallen short of Your Glory, for which You have cursed our nations with drought and pestilence and have opened our borders to the plunder of foreigners who do not know You. Even with the obvious signs in the stars, moon, sky and weather, we have not repented and returned our nations to You Lord in corporate repentance. Instead, our leaders have vowed to rebuild out of their own false sense of strength, thus raising a fist in defiance to Your Judgments.

Master, please have Mercy on us. We beg for Your Grace and Mercy. We are underserving of Your Mercy but Your Holy Word says you are patient, kind, loving, merciful and longsuffering. Please, because of who *You* are not because of what *we* are, hear our prayer and grant our petition this day. We know You will hear from Heaven and will forgive our sins and heal our lands if we humble ourselves, pray, seek Your Face and *turn* from our wicked ways.

Then may all the kingdoms of the world truly know that You are God and that there is no other God but You, the God of the Old and New Testaments, Almighty God over all. Any others are pretenders to the throne. May You get all the glory, honor and praise. May Your Kingdom come and may Your will be done on Earth as it is in Heaven. We pray this prayer with great expectancy, looking upwards for our Salvation when You will return to set things right forever and ever.

WE PRAY THIS PRAYER IN THE NAME OF JESUS CHRIST/YESHUA, THE NAME ABOVE ALL NAMES, THE KING OF KINGS AND THE LORD OF LORDS.
~Amen

DAY #1
Open Heavens ~ Let it Rain
Raise the Roof

40 Days of Rain

And many nations shall come, and say, Come, and LET US GO UP to the mountain of the LORD, to the House of the God of Jacob; and He will teach us of His ways, and we will walk in His paths: for the Law shall go forth of Zion, and the Word of the LORD from Jerusalem.
> ~ Micah 4:2 (KJV, emphasis added)

While pride is a fleshly, evil attempt at "getting to the top," repentance is the God-given practice approved by Jesus Christ Himself.

From that time Jesus began to preach and to say, "Repent, for the Kingdom of Heaven is at hand." ~ Matthew 4:17 (NKJV)

"Making Aliyah" is a phrase that describes the modern-day process of the Jews returning to the State of Israel. There is a spiritual concept of this process as well. The word *"aliyah"* means: "to go up," "to ascend," and more literally "stairway chamber" or "upper room." In ancient Jewish homes when they said: "Let us go up to pray"...they literally meant "Let us go up to the roof chamber" or "let us go *upstairs.*" Peter went UP to the rooftop to pray when he had his vision. God is still often referred to as "the Man upstairs."

We see this concept originally in the story of Jacob's Ladder. When Jacob had his vision, he saw angels ascending and descending a ladder. A ladder, also seen in many ancient Mid-eastern homes, represents the symbolic connection between earth and open heavens.

How does this pertain to the Church today?

The number one sin we must combat is pride. In the list of the "Seven Things the Lord Hates," this sin makes the top of the list. Until we grasp a deep understanding of how prideful we are, we will continue to be corrupted. As *individuals* we see this pride perversion in "Pride Parades" and as *nations* we see nationalistic "Patriotic Pride" taking precedence over national humiliation before God.

> The Tower of Babel builders sought to build themselves a city, *"and a tower whose top is in the Heavens; let us make a name for ourselves."*
> ~ Genesis 11:4. (NKJV, emphasis added)

This sounds suspiciously similar to Satan's attempt to overtake God's Throne found in Isaiah:

> *I will ascend above the heights of the clouds, I will be like the Most High.* ~ Isaiah 14:14 (ERV)

Pride is Satan's version of attempting to "go up." Repentance is God's approved method. It is the opposite of pride. It is a *key* given to us by God Almighty.

> *From the days of John the Baptist until now, the Kingdom of Heaven has been subject to violence, and the violent lay claim to it.* ~Matthew 11:12 (Berean Study Bible)

Jesus established a powerful reign among men requiring an essential reaction. So, how do we lay claim to the Kingdom of Heaven in a manner approved by God? In Judges 3:25, we see the very first time the word *"Key"* is mentioned in scripture. It referred to an inner chamber.

They waited to the point of embarrassment, but when he did
not open the doors of the room, they took a <u>key</u> and unlocked
them. ~Judges 3:25 (NIV, emphasis added)

Repentance is the Key that unlocks the door to the upper chamber.
Instead of attempting to reach Heaven by our own efforts, thereby
building another Tower of Babel, we must instead reach the "point of
embarrassment." When the doors of Heaven seem locked, we need to
become disgusted and humiliated with our sin. This dissatisfaction and
acknowledgement of our sinful state is the key with which we are able
to open the door to answer Jesus' knock!

> *Behold, I stand at the door and knock. If anyone should hear*
> *My voice <u>and open the door,</u> then I will come in to him and will*
> *dine with him, and he with Me.*
> ~ Revelation 3.20 (Berean Literal Bible, emphasis added)

Thus, we "go up," or "make Aliyah" by *getting down* on our knees! Christ
Himself has given us this key. Repentance, or spiritual Aliyah, is one of
the keys Jesus handed to the Church in order to enter the Kingdom of
Heaven.

> *I will give to you the keys of the kingdom of the heavens, and*
> *whatever you might bind on the earth shall have been bound in*
> *the heavens, and whatever you might loose on the earth shall*
> *have been loosed in the heavens.*
> ~ Matthew 16:19 (Berean Literal Bible)

So, let us "make Aliyah!" Let us go up by getting down on our knees
in humble prayer and repentance. In God's Kingdom, there is no "glass
ceiling." We may boldly approach the Throne of Grace. Repentance is
the God-given key that unlocks the door of our hearts to let Jesus in. Let
Him Reign!

Repentance Prayer:

Heavenly Father, I REPENT for my Pride. I have wanted to "go up" without "getting down" on my knees. Help me not to attempt to build another Tower of Babel by trying to storm Heaven in an ungodly manner. Teach us that the first Key to the Kingdom is humility. Help me to see that I am a drowning man, totally dependent upon you to save me. I now call out to You in REPENTANCE and adopt Your Truth from scripture. I acknowledge that without You, I can do nothing of any lasting value. Send the latter rains as we look onward to Your coming Reign. Thank You for helping us to get prepared. Strengthen us to follow through in obedience. We pray this prayer in the Name of Jesus Christ, the Name above all names, the King of kings, the Lord of lords and our Lord. ~Amen.

Scriptures to help me cleanse with His Word:

_____

_____

_____

DAY #2
Let's Call It a Night
Right as Rain

40 Nights of Rain

The night is nearly over; the day has drawn near. So let us lay
aside the deeds of darkness and put on the armor of light.
~ Romans 13:12 (Berean Study Bible)

The second sin mentioned in the "Seven Things That the Lord Hates" (Proverbs 6) is "a lying tongue."

In 1997, Jim Carrey starred in a move entitled; "Liar, Liar." While the overall story line was not something I can recommend viewing, the premise of the movie was quite hilarious. What if you or I were unable to lie? What if every time we opened our mouth, the Truth was the only thing that would come out? Would our lives look much different than they already are, or would this suddenly cause a complete shake-up all around us?

It seems today that Truth is not very popular. In fact, it would not be a stretch to say that lying has reached epidemic proportions in our culture and has garnered broad-based acceptance as the norm. Sadly we no longer expect our politicians or the news media to tell us the Truth.

Abraham Lincoln is reported to have said:

"You can fool some of the people all of the time, and all of the people some of the time, but you cannot fool all of the people all of the time."

I'm sure President Lincoln wasn't advocating lying. He was simply making an important observation. Most people will eventually realize when they are fed lies as a consistent diet. Let's just hope it is not too late.

Jesus tells us what He thinks of lies:

> You belong to your father, the devil, and you want to carry out your father's desire. He was a murderer from the beginning, not holding to the Truth, for there is no Truth in him. When he lies, he speaks his native language, for he is a liar and the father of lies. ~ John 8:44 (NIV)

Let's call it what it is: Since the devil is the father of ALL lies, when we lie, we are sadly following in the footsteps of Satan! After the sin of pride, lying is the very next sin we need to throw overboard during our repentance time. The first person we need to stop lying to is ourselves.

> If we say that we have no sin, we deceive ourselves, and the Truth is not in us. ~ 1 John 1:8 (KJV)

Since Jesus is the Way, the Truth and the Life…it is horrifying to think that when we live a life of consistently lying…Jesus (the Truth) is not in us. Shudders!

When we are lying we are not relying on God. We are manipulating and deceiving, which is akin to witchcraft…an abomination unto our Holy God.

For some, it will be difficult to make this change at first. You will be shocked at how many "white lies" (no such thing) that have sneaked into your life even in towards those closest around you.

It has been said: "The Truth will set you free, but first it will make you miserable."

I think this is a humorous way of saying that, when some of us recognize how deeply entrenched this sin has become in our lives, we will experience intense godly sorrow.

So, let's REPENT of lying. Our Father is up above, not down below. Rely on Him to assist you and fill you with His Spirit of Truth. Let us tell the Truth, the whole Truth and nothing but the Truth…so help us God.

When it rains, He pours. He pours out His Spirit of Truth. In Him, there is no more darkness. He will "right" our "night."

Repentance Prayer:

Heavenly Father, those who worship You must worship You in spirit and in Truth. In Jesus' Powerful Name, I REPENT for all the times I failed to tell the Truth, even in the smallest of things. There is no such thing as "white lies"...they are ALL as black as night. Please forgive me for any way in which I have lied. I renounce that sin pattern, which I've used to try to advance myself and my desires dishonestly. I now see that ANY lying is wicked and from the evil one. Help me to be silent or to speak the Truth as Your ambassador. Help me fulfill your desire for us to be salt and light. I adopt Your example, Jesus, because You only spoke Truth. Let my "yes" be yes and my "no" be no, understanding that anything more comes from the evil one. Thank you for helping me through the Power of Your Holy Spirit. Amen.

Scriptures to help me cleanse with His Word:

_____

_____

_____

DAY #3
The Righteous Brothers
Share and Share Alike

40 Righteous in Sodom?

Righteousness exalts a nation, but sin is a disgrace to any people. ~ *Proverbs 14:34 (Berean Study Bible)*

Many times, people have said to me: "But Pastor, there seem to be so few people repenting."

"And he [Abraham] spoke to Him yet again and said, "Suppose there should be forty [righteous] found there? So He said, "I will not do it for the sake of forty." ~Genesis 18:29 (NKJV)

We all know the rest of the story; the Lord agreed that He would not destroy Sodom if only TEN righteous were found within it! We must not be discouraged by small numbers. By individually repenting, just a few of us can help stave off crushing Judgment in our nations.

One of the sin issues we need to remove is the slaughter of innocents. The scripture tells us the third thing that the Lord hates:

...hands that shed innocent blood..." ~ Proverbs 6:17(b) (NKJV)

The hands in our nations are full of blood. We kill children in (and now out!) of the womb and euthanize the disabled, sick and elderly. Despite sonograms that clearly show a living human being, we allow laws to kill innocent babies just seconds before or after birth. Our government then pays (with our tax dollars!) for that horrific "service." The LORD hates this stench of blood. When we are praying with bloody hands, He will not hear our prayers:

> *When you spread out your hands, I will hide my eyes from*
> *you; Even though you make many prayers, I will not hear: Your*
> *hands are full of blood.* ~Isaiah 1:15 (NKJV)

Yet, there is a profound spiritual issue at stake here also. How do we continue to "slaughter innocents" in the spiritual world? Today let's take a deeper look at the story of Sodom and Gomorrah. The original story of its destruction is found in Genesis 19, but it is mentioned again in Ezekiel 16.

> *Behold, this was the iniquity of thy sister Sodom, pride, fullness*
> *of bread, and abundance of idleness was in her and in her*
> *daughters and neither did she strengthen the hand of the poor*
> *and needy.* ~ Ezekiel 16:49 (KJV)

Ezekiel was written during a time of bondage and captivity of ancient Israel while exiled in Babylon. What was the "iniquity" of Sodom? Most people would, of course, point to homosexuality. While homosexuality is most certainly a serious perversion of God's Holy order and plan, it was a symptom of a greater disease. What was the disease that caused the symptom of homosexuality?

Let's explain by understanding the meaning of the name "Sodom."

The name Sodom literally means "burning." We all know that Sodom was destroyed by fire, but Strong's Concordance states that this name came about because Sodom was built on bituminous soil due to its many previous fires. Bitumin is created by a heated refining process and is added to sandy soil (slippery footing) to increase stabilization. Thus we might say that the many "burnings," or great revival periods in our history, have helped to re-stabilize our slippery slope downward, at least temporarily.

In Ezekiel, God is prophetically admonishing those that have "lived in ease" and have not shared the Bread of Life with others as commanded. The sin that God is so angry about in Ezekiel 16 is not the "sin of inhospitality," it is the sin of a hardened people who were given abundant spiritual Bread yet squandered it all away in selfish living. It is a prophetic pre-shadowing of our own nations which, by not sharing the gospel message with the rest of the world (the poor and needy), we have instead encouraged abominations.

Western Civilization, greatly blessed by God Almighty, has actually endorsed: abortion, homosexuality, secularism and anti-GOD thinking throughout the world. Truly this is a horrible sin! We have been given many blessings by God Almighty and, in return, we have "refused to share." Instead, we have been abundant in eating the bread of idleness... lazy and wicked servants, indeed!

We now import sodomy to third world nations through our "rainbow diplomacy," birth control and abortion to poor countries to limit their growth, and a "no particular God" philosophy which encourages false, persecuting, demon-inspired religions to flourish. We may constantly pray for "revival" but revival fires will not come unless we repent first of these national sins.

Will the next Holy Spirit fire that is coming re-stabilize us or send us into exile? That depends on whether or not we repent. If we, as a nation, are grieved by the low estate brought about by our national sins, perhaps we can regain our footing.

Holy Spirit-filled Repentance is the only re-stabilization process that can bring this sinking sand back to solid ground.

Repentance Prayer:

Heavenly Father, I REPENT for any way that I have assisted in the shedding of innocent blood. I turn away from my apathy in allowing innocents to be slaughtered both physically and spiritually. I repent for participating in government programs that fund this evil and for failing to protest the practices of my nation which encourage living souls to be lost in sin. You have come to bring LIFE and LIFE more abundantly. You told us to be fruitful and multiply. I now adopt Your requirement to respect all human LIFE from natural conception to natural death and to only support man/woman marriage which creates Life. You are Life itself. Forgive me for violating and perverting those created in Your Holy Image. Teach me to walk in Your path of righteousness for Your Name's sake and to share Your life with all others. Thank you for helping me. In Jesus' Name I pray. ~ Amen

Scriptures to help me cleanse with His Word:

_____

_____

_____

DAY #4
Going to the Chapel
I'll be His and He'll be Mine

40 Years of Age When Isaac Married Rebekah

Come hither, I will shew thee the bride, the Lamb's wife.
~ Revelation 21:9 (b) (KJV)

Isaac was 40-years old when he married Rebekah. Forty years of waiting in the desert must have seemed like a lifetime. According to scripture, she was a woman of extraordinary beauty (Genesis 24:16) with a humble servant's attitude (Genesis 24:18-20)....,well worth the wait.

Notice Rebekah's reply when asked if she would go with Abraham's servant, Eliezer, to wed Isaac. It sounds very much like a wedding vow:

And they called Rebekah, and said unto her, Wilt thou go with
this man? And she said, "I will go."   *~ Genesis 24:58 (KJV)*

Rebekah was obedient. She followed God's plans, not her own.

We need to be like Rebekah, a great biblical role model. One of the sin issues we need to remove is any residue of devising our own plans, for our own glory instead of following the Lord's calling. The scripture tells us the fourth thing that the Lord hates:

...a heart that devises wicked plans..."
~ Proverbs 6:18(a) (NKJV)

The Lord calls us to abhor a heart that devises rebellious plans. We are to be guileless, humble and servile. We are to use any physical advantages He created in us to worship Him and to advance His Kingdom by following His Path of Righteousness. We must say: "I will go, Lord."

Rebellion against God's plan is at the root of anyone devising wicked plans. We remove this sin stronghold by repentance and by the washing of the Word.

Now, under His Blood, we can become righteous: Holy as He is holy. Thanks to Jesus, now our hearts can express His love. Instead of devising our own plans and spreading more evil, we can put our hearts towards following Him and loving others.

Repentance Prayer:

Heavenly Father, I REPENT for any way in which I have planned evil by following my own way. I repent for allowing selfish thoughts to take root in my mind and cause me to embrace any other plan than Yours. The scripture teaches us that planned or willful sins are "presumptuous" sins and cause us to be guilty of great transgression if we allow them to have dominion over us. (Psalm 19:13). Help me now to HATE rebellious plans and to LOVE righteousness. Help me to walk in Your pathways for Your Name's sake. Teach me to share Your Love and Goodness with others. Thank you for helping me overcome sin. I pray in Jesus' Name. ~ Amen

Scriptures to help me cleanse with His Word:

_____

_____

_____

DAY #5
Unholy Matrimony
Unequally Yoked?

40 Years Old When Esau Took a Wife

*And no one pours new wine into old wineskins. If he does, the
wine will burst the skins, and both the wine and the wineskins
will be ruined. Instead, new wine is poured into new wineskins.*
~ Mark 2:22 (Berean Study Bible)

The scripture tells us the fifth thing that the Lord hates:

Feet that are quick to rush into evil..."
~ Proverbs 6:18(b) (NIV)

In our previous Repentance Devotional, we outlined the obedience of
Rebekah in submitting to God's Plan in her marriage to Isaac, the child
of promise. Today we discuss the disobedience of Esau in marrying two
foreign wives.

*When Esau was forty years old, he took as his wives Judith
daughter of Beeri the Hittite and Basemath daughter of Elon
the Hittite.* *~ Genesis 26:34 (Berean Study Bible)*

The next scripture verse is often overlooked. The verse that immediately
follows Esau's disobedience is this one:

And they brought grief to Isaac and Rebekah.
                    ~ Genesis 26:35 (Berean Study Bible)

Another often overlooked fact is that Esau (meaning "redness" or "earthiness"...Human thinking instead of God's wisdom) marries again for a third time! Apparently, attempting to get it right on Wife #3, he marries within the Hebrew family...yet this too is a disaster.

Esau went to Ishmael and married Mahalath, the sister of Nebaioth and daughter of Abraham's son Ishmael, in addition to the wives he already had.
                    ~ Genesis 28:9 (Berean Study Bible)

His third Bride's name, Mahalath, roughly translated means *"diseased Hebrew dance."* (source: Abarim Publications)

Ancient Rabbinical Commentary also supports this view in a Midrash:

"Esau did not mend his ways and Mahalath was as evil as his first two wives (Midrash Aggadah, ed. Buber, Gen 28:9). This later marriage was also the result of negative motives: Esau plotted together with Ishmael to kill Isaac and Jacob, to marry the daughter of Ishmael, and to inherit both families. Accordingly, his marriage to Mahalath was "ke-mahalah" (as an affliction) and only increased the pain his parents had suffered upon his first marriages   (Gen. Rabbah 67:8, 13)."

Yeshua/Jesus sees His believers as His Bride. He is the soon-returning Bridegroom. To be a part of His Bride, we have to repent and believe that He is the Christ of the Living God, The Messiah.   (Matthew 4:17).

There is a movement that calls us to go back to old Hebrew traditions and roots, as if by participating in the festivals alone is sufficient and that Yeshua/Jesus doesn't have to be central.

While it is perfectly fine to point out the stunning Old Testament prophecies that were fulfilled in our Messiah Yeshua, we should NOT support a return to Old Covenant living. This would be a rush into an "Esau-type" wedding. While we may joyfully embrace our Hebrew roots, we must not do this by "marrying" old methods which do not recognize the fulfillment found in our Messiah Yeshua/Jesus Christ.

> *Jesus said: But whoever denies Me before men, I will also deny him before My Father in heaven.*
> *~ Matthew 10:33 (Berean Study Bible)*

And He further said:

> *If anyone is ashamed of Me and My words, the Son of Man will be ashamed of him when He comes in His glory and in the glory of the Father and of the holy angels.*
> *~Luke 9:26 (Berean Study Bible)*

Paul the Apostle, when preaching in the Jewish synagogues clearly *named* Jesus Christ the Messiah:

> *This Jesus, Whom I proclaim to you, is the Christ (the Messiah).*
> *~Acts 17:3 (b) (ESV)*

Scripture makes a clear distinction between "rushing" and "*hurrying*." Rushing is an evil concept but hurrying is a godly one (one such example is 1 Samuel 17:48 NKJV). We cannot "rush" God's Sovereign Plan, but as ambassadors of His Peace, let's hurry to proclaim His Name.

> *In freedom Christ has set us free. Stand firm, therefore and do not be entangled again in a yoke of slavery!*
> *~ Galatians 5:1 (Berean Literal Bible)*

Repentance Prayer

Heavenly Father, Forgive me for any way in which, like Esau, I have rushed into evil. Keep me from committing the same sins as Esau by utilizing humanistic thinking instead of Your Godly wisdom. Let us not think that we have a better method of "marrying" Yeshua to Your people than the simple gospel message. Fill us with Your Holy Spirit power to give us the BOLDNESS of Peter, John and Paul to declare the need for CHRIST and CHRIST CRUCIFIED, no matter how many people prefer us to not speak Your Holy Name. Let us not attempt to pour New Wine into old wineskins. We pray in the Power of the Name above all names, the Lord of lords, the King of kings. This Name is Yeshua, the Prince of Peace, under which every knee shall bow and every tongue confess that HE IS LORD. ~ Amen

Scriptures to help me cleanse with His Word:

_____

_____

DAY #6
Walking Straight and True
Path-O-Logical?

40 Days Israel (Jacob) was embalmed in
Egypt before buried in Canaan

*A false witness shall perish: but the man that heareth (discerns)
speaketh constantly.* ~Proverbs 21:28 (KJV)

In Genesis 50, Joseph embalms his father, Israel, for forty days in order to take his body back to the Promised Land for a final burial in the Cave of the Patriarchs. Jacob's name was changed to Israel because he *"wrestled with God and with men" and won!* (Genesis 32:28/CEV)

As many stories in the Bible are, at first glance this one appears to be very odd. Why embalm Israel according to *Egyptian* customs instead of burying him according to Hebrew customs?

It seems, the "logical path" would have been for Joseph to continue following Hebrew customs. However, Joseph was no fool. He had to carry his father's body back to Canaan which was probably a 30-40 day road trip. He would have had a rotting corpse on his hands.

For today's devotional, the scripture tells us the SIXTH thing that the Lord hates:

A false witness who speaks lies.." Proverbs 6:19(a) (NKJV)

Pastor Jeffrey Daly

A "false witness" is one that impugns the character of an undeserving person. If you or I were on a witness stand, and we were asked to "tell the Truth, the whole Truth and nothing but the Truth, so help me God," we would NOT be "bearing false witness" simply because someone's reputation was ruined. If someone committed a crime, Justice would demand that the Truth still be told.

The Holy Scripture tells us that a person who bears false witness will perish. However, it also tells us that he who hears (discerns) from God speaks constantly with wisdom.

Like Joseph, we must not always follow what often seems to be the most obvious way. When it comes to bringing our family and friends into the Promised Land, keeping our mouth shut may seem like the "logical path." However, it never is when it comes to testifying against falsity within the church. The Lord calls us to walk straight and true. We are to speak the Way, the Truth and the Life. Anything less and we will have a decaying Body on our hands.

Repentance Prayer:

Heavenly Father, Please teach me when to speak and when to remain silent. Help me to discern what is true and what is false. Help me to not only walk straight but true. Please forgive me for any time I failed to tell the Truth. I REPENT for any time that I have been the bearer of a false witness. Please embolden me instead to declare the Truth of Your Holy Word. We pray this prayer in the Name of Jesus Christ/ Yeshua, the Name above all names, the King of kings and the Lord of Lords. ~ Amen

Scriptures to help me cleanse with His Word:

_____

_____

_____

DAY #7
Sowing Bad Seed
Fear the Reaper

40 Years Moses lived in Egypt before the Exodus

Then another angel came out of the temple, crying out in a loud voice to the One seated on the cloud, "Swing Your sickle and reap, because the time has come to harvest; for the crop of the earth is ripe."

~ Revelation 14:15 (Berean Study Bible)

For Day #7 of our Repentance Devotionals, we come upon another fascinating Bible story. It appears Moses was 40-years old before he decided to visit his Hebrew brethren.

Despite many Hollywood dramatizations, the scripture does not tell us how or when Moses knew that he was a Hebrew. Perhaps he always knew it, or perhaps it was a slowly growing awareness.

Nevertheless, when he was 40-years old, he decided he wanted to rediscover his Hebrew roots. When he went to where the Jews were laboring, he happened upon an Egyptian beating a Hebrew. Moses then killed the Egyptian and buried his body in the sand.

Moses probably originally felt like a "savior" to his people but was surprised, instead, to find them calling him out on murder. When this news reached Pharaoh, he had to run for his life into the desert for another forty years!

There is a SEVENTH thing the Lord hates....

....one who sows discord among brethren.

Proverbs 6:19(b) (NKJV)

Christians and Jews are brethren in the same way that genetically born children and adopted children are siblings. We cannot rush in and "kill the Egyptian" (disdain our Christian history) thinking, that in doing so, we will become the new Savior of the Jews.

In a misguided attempt to liberate the Jews, we must not throw all of Christianity under the bus. We must not sow discord among brethren branches or we will be on the run from God's Judgment. We spiritually "slay" when we refuse to share the gospel message to the Jews, through the naming of Yeshua the Messiah, in a misguided attempt to create our own version of "peace."

Rightfully so, the Jews would then spiritually wonder at the genuineness of our purpose: *"Will you slay us also, like you slayed the Egyptian?"* ~ Exodus 2:14(b) (NKJV)

Sowing seeds of discord between Christianity and Messianic Judaism only serves the devil's purposes. It will place us on the back side of a desert with the goats, unusable for another forty years.

Let's repent for any legitimate abuses such as "replacement theology" that have come from the Gentile Christian world. On the other hand, let's not throw out the baby (the Christ child) with the bathwater (the heresies).

God will use all those who love and obey him to preach liberty to the entire world. We must not, in the meanwhile, imagine ourselves as the next Deliverer of the Jewish people without declaring who their Savior really is.

That honor belongs to One Person and One Person only...YESHUA, The Messiah.

The Deliverer will come out of Zion,
And He will turn away ungodliness from Jacob;
For this is My covenant with them,
When I take away their sins.

~Romans 11:26-27(b) (NKJV)

Repentance Prayer

Heavenly Father, Forgive me for any way in which I have rebelled against You and have failed to preach Christ in a desire to be more popular with men. All authority in heaven and on earth has been given to You, Lord Jesus. Forgive me for acting in disobedience to You and failing to trust in Your Holy Name.

Help me to REPENT to receive Your Love and to replace my stronghold of rebellion. Teach me to obey You and to spread Your love as Your ambassador. I want to be zealous to repent and to dine with You, to be an overcomer of any seed of rebellion. I want to bless others with the same Gift of Jesus Christ/Yeshua that I have been blessed with, teaching that there is no lasting peace without the Prince of Peace.

I pray in the Power of the Name above all names, the Lord of lords, the King of kings: Yeshua the Prince of Peace under which every knee shall bow and every tongue confess that HE IS LORD.
~ Amen

Scriptures to help me cleanse with His Word:

_____

_____

_____

Pastor Jeffrey Daly

DAY # 8
Take Off Your Shoes
Waiting for the Other Shoe to Drop

40 More Years Moses Lived in the
Wilderness before Exodus

*The LORD is near to the brokenhearted; He saves the contrite
in spirit.*

Psalm 34:18 (Berean Study Bible)

In our last seven Repentance Devotionals we examined the "Seven things the Lord hates." For the next seven days we will concentrate on "The Seven Deadly Sins." Once again, Pride tops the list.

For the first forty years of his life, Moses lived as a prince in Egypt. Then, for the next forty years of his life, he lived as a shepherd in the wilderness. Moses was a "shadow and type" of our Deliverer, the Lord Jesus Christ.

In these eighty years of training, Moses, like Yeshua, had experienced two extremes...highly exalted and then greatly humbled. These two extremes were necessary training for him to usher the Chosen People into the Promised Land.

Moses got to walk prophetically in Yeshua's shoes yet, before God at the Burning Bush, he took off his own shoes.

We see a similar pattern with John the Baptist:

> *John answered all of them: "I baptize you with water, but One more powerful than I will come, the straps of whose sandals I am not worthy to untie. He will baptize you with the Holy Spirit and with fire.* ~ Luke 3:16 (Berean Study Bible)

Simply put, humility pleases God. It is no wonder that the #1 "Deadly Sin" on the sin hit parade is PRIDE, the opposite of humility. Our Lord and Savior humbled Himself to come down here and to walk awhile in our shoes.

> *Let this mind be in you which was also in Jesus: Who existing in the form of God, did not consider equality with God something to be grasped, but emptied Himself, taking the form of a servant, being made in human likeness. And being found in appearance as a man, He humbled Himself and became obedient to death—even death on a cross.*
> ~ Philippians 2: 5-8 (Berean Study Bible)

The Lord is the same today as He was in Moses' time. He will be the same tomorrow and forever. He has an assignment, a calling for you and me, as He had for Moses. What is your assignment? Are you and I listening to Him daily, waiting for His instructions? As we humble ourselves through daily repentance, we will hear His Voice, and He will give us His grace. Whether we are in a time of high exaltation or on the backside of the wilderness, we must always be prepared to move onward.

Repentance Prayer:

Heavenly Father, You are Holy. I kneel, taking off my shoes, asking Your forgiveness and humbling myself before You. Forgive me for any way in which I have failed to listen to You out of my own pride. Forgive me for following old sin patterns out of my old way of thinking, acting in disobedience to You. I want to be prepared to take off my own shoes and walk in humility, in Your Way. Help me to obey You in whatever

circumstances I find myself, always being ready to move onward towards Your Promised Land. I want to be zealous to REPENT and to dine with You, to be an overcomer of any remnant of pride. I want to bless others, bearing with others in love while endeavoring to keep the unity of the Spirit in the bond of peace. We pray in the Power of the Name above all names, the Lord of lords, the King of kings, Yeshua. ~ Amen

Scriptures to help me cleanse with His Word:

_____

_____

_____

DAY #9

You Can't Always Get What You Want

Eaten Up With Envy

40 Years the Children of Israel Ate Manna

Do not let your heart envy sinners, But live in the fear of the LORD always.

~ Proverbs 23:17 (NASB)

"How much is enough?"...the famous saying goes...*"Just a little bit more."*...is the very telling answer.

If there is anything redeeming about reality TV (which I often sincerely doubt), it might actually be useful as an object lesson. It allows us to watch wealthy and famous people who, by the world's standards "have it all," remain *utterly miserable.* In recent years, there seems to be more suicides and early deaths than ever before by so-called "stars" and "celebrities."

For today's Devotional we discuss #2 on the list of "The Seven Deadly Sins"...Envy. Don't think you are exempt from repenting of this sin even if you don't crave material things. The church is full of envy for others' spiritual blessings as well.

This was the exact problem for the Israelites as they wandered in the wilderness. While God was supplying them with miraculous manna from Heaven, they craved after the Egyptian's spices:

"We remember the fish we ate freely in Egypt, along with the cucumbers, melons, leeks, onions, and garlic."
~ Numbers 11:5 (Berean Study Bible)

To put this in the correct context: We must remember that they were in *bondage as slaves* in Egypt! What a selective memory!

Initially God gave them what they wanted. However, be careful what you wish for. He gave them so much meat in the form of flying quail that they were literally choking on it. Isn't that exactly what is sadly happening to many rich and famous people?

One thing we know for sure:

More is not necessarily better.

Let's REPENT for constantly wanting what others have. Envy can only be removed by cultivating a spirit of generosity. Instead of focusing on what you don't have, start finding ways to bless others with what they need.

Repentance Prayer

Heavenly Father, Forgive me for any way in which I have envied others. Forgive me for following old sin patterns of my flesh and of the secular world. Help me to REPENT to receive Your Love and replace any remaining strongholds of envy. Help me to obey You and to spread a spirit of generosity as Your ambassador. I have no reason to envy because I have the greatest treasure in the Universe...the gift of Salvation from our Lord and Savior Jesus Christ. I want to be zealous to repent and to dine with You, to be an overcomer of any trace of envy for earthly things. Help me to march onward as a Christian soldier, blessing others, and building up treasure in Heaven instead of on earth where moths and rust corrupt. I pray in the Power of the Name above all names, the Lord of lords, the King of kings, Yeshua, the Giver of all good and perfect gifts. ~ Amen

Scriptures to help me cleanse with His Word:

_____

_____

_____

Pastor Jeffrey Daly

DAY #10

Anger Management
It's All the Rage

40 Years the Israelites Wandered in the Wilderness

Be ye angry, and sin not: let not the sun go down upon your wrath: Neither give place to the devil.

~Ephesians 4:26-27 (KJV)

Moses shows us a classic example of the sin of wrath. When the Israelites were wandering in the wilderness, Moses struck the rock twice in a fit of rage because of their constant complaining. God was angry with Moses and said he would not be able to enter the Promised Land for this action. This must be a very serious sin if it kept Moses out of the Promised Land!

In today's Devotional we discuss the third deadly sin of anger or wrath. First, what exactly is "wrath." Doesn't God pour out His Wrath in scripture? If so, how can it be a deadly sin since God does not sin?

First we must understand that God's Wrath is JUST. He is perfect and His Judgments are perfect. We are not perfect, therefore, we don't have the holy right to pour out wrath on others. We are not to condemn people, but instead offer them grace through Christ Jesus.

Furthermore, God's wrath is against sin. He gives us the way to avoid His Wrath by deliverance through His Son Jesus Christ.

And to wait for his Son from heaven, whom he raised from the dead, even Jesus, which delivered us from the wrath to come.
~ 1 Thessalonians 1:10 (KJV)

To say this another way: God's Wrath must be appeased. *He appeased it HIMSELF.* All who avail themselves of this Gift will be spared the holy wrath to come. Hallelujah. Thank you Yeshua!

This is why our personal wrath is such a deadly sin. Wrath kills. Many of us may have not killed a person in cold blood, but in taking vengeance and failing to control our anger, we have killed relationships and our Christian witness. Even worse, we are attempting to put ourselves in a final Judgment Seat where only God belongs...a truly Luciferian move.

Prophetically, Moses represents the Law and Joshua represents Yeshua. The Law will never allow us to cross over into the Promised Land...only Yeshua enables us to do so! This is a spiritual battle. Repentance can remove that enemy stronghold and replace it with God's Truth.

Let's stop "wandering in the wilderness "of our sin. Repent of any uncontrolled rage and anger issues so you may "enter in."

Repentance Prayer:

Heavenly Father, Forgive me for any way in which I have tried to take vengeance and spewed my wrath on others. I REPENT for not using Your Word to take down this stronghold of wrath in my soul. Forgive me for following old sin patterns out of my old way of thinking, acting in disobedience to You. Help me to repent daily to receive Your Love to replace any stronghold of vengeance and wrath. I replace it with Your Love through Your Holy Spirit in me. Help me to obey You and to spread Your Love as Your ambassador. I want to be zealous to repent and to dine with You, to be an overcomer of any seed of wrath. I want to bless others, witnessing Your Love to them. I pray in the Name of Jesus Christ/Yeshua, who came to spare us from the punishment of sin by trusting in Him. ~Amen

Scriptures to help me cleanse with His Word:

_____

_____

_____

DAY #11
Power Dressing
Wearing Out Your Welcome

40 Years the Garments of the
Israelites Did Not Wear Out

And he answered and spake unto those that stood before him,
saying, Take away the filthy garments from him. And unto him
he said, Behold, I have caused thine iniquity to pass from thee,
and I will clothe thee with change of raiment.

~ Zechariah 3:4 (KJV)

The fourth Deadly Sin is SLOTH.

Sloth is sometimes defined as laziness but it is also defined as "a failure to do the things one should do."

Zeal is the virtue opposing sloth. Therefore, when we are slothful, there is no zeal which is a key necessary ingredient in repentance. We can have no good works without zeal; and without good works, the scripture tells us we have no faith...a very serious spiritual condition.

In fact, the very term "faith alone" is not found in scripture. The only verse where "faith" and "alone" are found together is this one:

Even so faith, if it hath not works, is dead, being alone.

~ James 2:17 (KJV, emphasis added)

When researching the topic for this devotional, I came across a humorous meme. It stated:

"Sloth...the sin that needs no effort."

I guess that's really not all that funny...that we can sin by doing nothing!

In the wilderness, God supernaturally maintained the clothing of the Israelites so that their garments and their sandals did not wear out for forty years. Spiritually, God has clothed us with garments of righteousness and has shod our feet with the gospel of peace so that we will be able to complete the journey.

Thus, we have no excuse for laziness. In Revelation, Jesus, the Risen Christ admonishes the church that has had previous good works, but is now slothful and lazy, to go back to their first love.

> *Remember therefore from where you have fallen, and repent, and do the first works. But if not, I am coming to you, and I will remove your lampstand out of its place, unless you should repent.*
> ~ Revelation 2:5 (Berean Literal Bible)

Jesus reminds us that passion and repentance require zeal. So let's be zealous to repent so that we are properly clothed in His righteousness.

> *Those who I love, I reprove and discipline, so be zealous and repent.* ~ Revelation 3:19 (ESV)

Repentance Prayer

Heavenly Father, Forgive me for any way in which I have been slothful and apathetic. Energize me to walk in the good works that you have already prepared for me to do. Fill me with the power of Your Holy Spirit to enable me to do all things through Christ who strengthens me. Fill me with your passion and zeal to REPENT so that I may dine with You and be an overcomer of any seed of slothfulness. Clothe me in Your Righteous Garments, so graciously already provided by You. Your garment does not wear out and You will help us to arrive properly dressed into the Promised Land. We pray in the Name of Yeshua our Deliverer, Savior, Messiah and Bridegroom. ~ Amen

Scriptures to help me cleanse with His Word:

_____

_____

_____

DAY #12
Holy Cow
On the Horns of a Dilemma

40 Days Moses Was Getting the
Law Tablets the First Time

*And Jesus answering said unto them, Render to Caesar the
things that are Caesar's, and to God the things that are God's.
And they marveled at Him*

~ Mark 12:17 (KJV)

For today's devotional, let us consider the fifth Deadly Sin of Greed.

When Moses went up to Mount Sinai to get the commandments the first
time, he was up there for forty days. When he came down the mountain,
carrying the two tablets, which contained the ten commandments, he
heard quite a commotion coming from the camp.

Joshua, Moses' attendant, said that the noise was war, but Moses
recognized that the raised voices were actually *singing*! They were singing
praises to the false god that they created!

Now, you may ask, what does this have to do with repenting of greed?
Join me as we contemplate this scripture verse carefully.

> *Then Moses returned to the Lord and said, "Oh, these people
> have committed a great sin, and have made for themselves a
> god of gold.*   ~ Exodus 32:31 (NKJV)

Interestingly, the modern day money symbol on Wall Street very much resembles a "golden calf." Jesus told us that we cannot serve two masters. We will love one and hate the other. Notice He didn't simply say: We will love one and disregard the other. We will HATE the other. Can you imagine a church that hates Jesus Christ? Once the church turns over to serving Mammon, it will automatically follow that they are at odds with Jesus Christ Himself. Soon enough they will find themselves at war with God Almighty while singing praises to Mammon. No wonder we sometimes refer to money as "the Almighty Dollar"...this idol worship is something we need to repent of!

Another fact that is also often overlooked is that Aaron, the high priest of Israel, actually made the calf himself! Aaron represents the spiritual leadership of the nation. Let's look at Aaron's response:

> So I said to them, "Whoever has gold, let him take it off," and
> they gave it to me. And when I cast it into the fire, out came
> this calf!"   ~ Exodus 32:24 (Berean Study Bible)

According to Aaron, it seems that in the very act of donating only gold as a sacrifice...a golden calf automatically pops out. Interesting. The God who already owns all the cattle on the hills doesn't need our money, He wants our heart, soul and mind participation.

So, what is all the commotion in our camps? Just who and what are we "singing our praises" to?

It's time to REPENT. No bull.

Repentance Prayer:

Heavenly Father, Help us to root out the sin of GREED from our lives. Teach us to not demand a god of gold but a God of Good. Help us to encourage a spirit of charity and generosity as a spiritual antidote to this sin. As we REPENT, let us acknowledge how closely related many of these sins are. Greed is dependent upon envy, covetousness, pride, gluttony and lust also. Help us to get at the root of these sins

and submit to You in plucking out these dangerous weeds that seek to choke out fruit. Forgive me for any way in which the spirit of greed has kept me from You. Fill me with Your passion and zeal to repent so that I may dine with You and be an overcomer of any seed of greed. You are our Provider and You are our Joy. We pray in the name of Yeshua, Who gives us the only lasting and eternal treasure. ~ Amen

Scriptures to help me cleanse with His Word:

_____

_____

_____

DAY #13
Can't Get No Satisfaction
Breaking Bad

40 Days for Moses to Obtain the
Law Tablets a Second Time

*I will give you a new heart and put a new spirit within you; I
will remove your heart of stone and give you a heart of flesh.*
~ Ezekiel 36:26 (Berean Study Bible)

I find it wryly humorous that even secular song lyrics often cluelessly affirm God's Truth. Jesus said that if His People didn't bring Him glory, even the stones would cry out.

*"I tell you," He answered, "if they remain silent, the very stones
will cry out."* ~ Luke 19:40 (Berean Study Bible)

In the song lyrics of today's title, we have an example of the "Stones" crying out, the Rolling Stones (yes, pun intended!). In their anthem song screed about the dissatisfaction of a godless humanistic lifestyle, they unintentionally affirm a scriptural Truth. We "can't get no satisfaction" from worldly pursuits. That's because hell is never satisfied.

*Hell and Destruction are never full; So the eyes of man are
never satisfied.* ~ Proverbs 27:20 (KJV)

For today's devotional, let us consider the sixth Deadly Sin of Gluttony. The overall prevailing sin of the Israelites in the wilderness was their constant complaining that they wanted something "more."

They were, in essence, saying that God Almighty was not enough for them. This is the same God who saved them from slavery, parted the Red Sea, destroyed the Egyptian army, miraculously fed them in the desert and divinely maintained their clothing and sandals.

Apparently, this all-providing God was not enough for their gluttonous souls. Moses was so angered upon seeing their betrayal that he smashed the ten commandment tablets to the ground in fury after his first forty days on Mount Sinai.

> As Moses approached the camp and saw the calf and the dancing, he burned with anger and threw the tablets out of his hands, smashing them at the base of the mountain.
> ~ Exodus 32:19 (Berean Study Bible)

Few people realize that Moses had to spend another forty days on Mount Sinai to get the second set of stone commandments.

How do we avoid this grievous sin of gluttony? We must begin by being thankful and, we must also stop complaining. We have so much that God has given to us and we are truly blessed beyond comprehension. Our modern lifestyles today would have been the envy of kings past. Clearly satisfaction is not about the abundance of "things."

Some people claim this Rolling Stones song has a downbeat that is the opposite of a natural heartbeat. I don't know if this is really true, but it still strikes a chord. Unless we fill our hearts with the satisfaction that can only come from Christ...we will continue to be off-beat.

Repentance Prayer:

Heavenly Father, Help us to root out the sin of GLUTTONY from our lives. Teach us to be satisfied with You and the provision from Your Hand. Help us to develop the virtue of contentment as a spiritual antidote to this sin. As we REPENT, let us acknowledge how closely related many of these sins are as gluttony is dependent upon envy, covetousness, pride, greed and lust also. Fill me with your passion and zeal to repent so that I may dine with You and be an overcomer of any seed of gluttony. You are my Provider and my Joy. Help me to be satisfied in You. We pray in the Name of Yeshua, the only eternally satisfying Gift who teaches us to require nothing more. ~ Amen

Scriptures to help me cleanse with His Word:

_____

_____

_____

DAY #14
The Spy Who Loves Me
Counter Intelligence

40 Years Old When Joshua Spied
Out the Promised Land

*But I tell you that anyone who looks at a woman to lust after
her has already committed adultery with her in his heart.*
~ Matthew 5:28 (Berean Study Bible)

LUST...the final and seventh Deadly Sin. Indeed, it is truly deadly as we have seen from the emotional fall-out in the Catholic Church pedophilia scandals. Let others in the Christian faith not look with pride on the Roman Catholic struggles, nor have this unrepentant attitude:

*The Pharisee stood by himself and prayed, 'God, I thank
You that I am not like the other men-swindlers, evildoers,
adulterers-or even like this tax collector.*
~ Luke 18:11 (Berean Study Bible)

The Truth is: We are just like these sinners unless we repent. The heart is desperately wicked, who can know it? Protestants have (and continue to have) their share of lust scandals. Let's not forget the Ashley Madison adultery scandal that reached the upper echelons of the pulpits. A recent poll showed that the majority of those in the ministry look at online porn at least once a week! REPENT!

*There is a generation of those who are pure in their own eyes
and yet unwashed of their filth.*
                    ~ Proverbs 30:12 (Berean Study Bible)

Clearly this is not "denomination specific"...it is an endemic problem and rampant in the churches today. Repentance has not been taught, let alone displayed, by too many pastors and priests. Judgment begins in the House of the Lord. I believe we are witnessing this judgement in the current news.

In today's 40/40's, we see that Joshua was forty years old when he was sent to spy out the Promised Land. Like many other figures in the Old Testament, Joshua is a shadow-type of Yeshua.

Joshua/Yeshua is searching the land to see *"whether the people who dwell in it are strong or week, few or many; whether the land they dwell in is good or bad; whether the cities they inhabit are like camps or strongholds; whether the land is rich or poor; and whether there be forests there or not."*
                    ~ Numbers 13:17-20(a) (NKJV)

This is prophetic. Christ is viewing the vineyards. The next scripture tells us what is up ahead:

Be of good courage. And bring some of the fruit of the land. Now the time was the season of the first ripe grapes.
                    ~ Exodus 13: 20(b) (NKJV)

While it may seem counter-intuitive based on the news accounts, Yeshua is still bringing back a good report. These giants of lust are no match for Him. NOW is the time. NOW is the season. REPENT and enter the Promised Land.

Repentance Prayer

Heavenly Father, Help us to remove the sin of LUST from our lives. Help us turn away from the flesh to find wholeness in Your indwelling Holy Spirit. Enable us to develop the virtue of chastity as a spiritual antidote to this sin. As we REPENT, let us acknowledge how closely related many of these sins are as lust is dependent upon envy, covetousness, pride, greed and gluttony also. Forgive me for any way in which the spirit of lust has kept me from You. Fill me with Your passion and zeal to repent so that I may dine with You and be an overcomer of any seed of lust. Guard my mind and my eyes. We pray in the Power of the Name above all names, the Lord of lords, the King of kings: Yeshua the Prince of Peace under which every knee shall bow and every tongue confess that HE IS LORD. ~ Amen

Scriptures to help me cleanse with His Word:

_____

_____

DAY #15
Command Center
Putting on the Dog

40 Days Joshua & Caleb Spied Out the Promised Land

Mephibosheth bowed down and said, "What is your servant, that you should show regard for a dead dog like me?"
~ 2 Samuel 9:8 (Berean Study Bible)

"Yes, Lord," she said, "even the dogs eat the crumbs that fall from their masters' table."
~ Matthew 15:27 (Berean Study Bible)

For the next ten devotionals we will be examining the ten commandments as we continue down our outline of the 40/40's.

In Numbers 13, Joshua and Caleb spied out the Promised Land for forty days. We have previously discussed how closely related the name Joshua is to Yeshua.

What few people know is that the name "Caleb" is identical to the Hebrew word בלכ (*keleb*), which means "dog." When you think about it, this is rather funny. It means that, along with the young children, only Yeshua and His loyal dog made it into the Promised Land!

Sadly, the other Israelites chose to believe the "bad report" instead of the "good report" from Joshua and Caleb. They did not believe that they could "take the land" from the giants, even after all of the miraculous help they had received from God Almighty up until this point.

Too often we have taken the ten commandments as the "ten suggestions" or "The ten great ideas no one can actually obey." Yet, Jesus clearly said:

Those who LOVE ME, KEEP MY COMMANDS.
~John 14:15 NIV

Whoever has My commandments and keeps them is the one who loves Me. The one who loves Me will be loved by My Father, and I will love him and reveal Myself to him."
~ John 14:21 (Berean Study Bible)

Furthermore, His commands are not grievous or burdensome (too difficult to adhere to or too heavy to bear).

For this is the love of God, that we should keep His commandments; and His commandments are not burdensome.
~ 1 John 5:3 (Berean Literal Bible)

Studies show that even dogs can remember ten simple commands!

So, let's make this very easy...All ten commandments can be applied to simple commands that even dogs readily learn:

#1) Sit: No other gods before Me.
#2) Drop it: No graven images
#3) No barking: Do not take the Lord's Name in vain
#4) Lie down: Remember the Sabbath
#5) Heel: Honor your mother and father
#6) Roll over: Do not murder
#7) Stay: Do not commit adultery
#8) Leave it: Do not steal
#9) Quiet: Don't bear false witness
#10) Wait: Don't covet

For today's devotional we are reminded to fully obey Commandment #1. We are instructed to place no other gods before the Lord. He is our Master.

The realization we must come to, like a loyal dog, is that the #1 "god" we most often have sitting up on our comfy couch throne is *ourselves*. We need to repent on bended knee for our disloyalty and disobedience.

Like Caleb, let's be obedient and...GET DOWN!

Repentance Prayer:

Heavenly Father, Today we acknowledge that Your commands are right and true and You expect us to make every effort to OBEY THEM. We begin at the beginning by making You the Lord of our lives. You are our Master and, at your side, we will enter into the Promised Land. Help us to put aside our own disobedient ways and follow You without question. We pray this prayer in the Name above all names, the King of kings, the Lord of lords, Yeshua: The Prince of Peace under which every knee (and paw!) must bow. ~ Amen

Scriptures to help me cleanse with His Word:

_____

_____

_____

DAY #16
Exit Strategy
Idle Worship

40 Chapters in the Book of Exodus

And the angel said unto me, Wherefore didst thou marvel? I will tell thee the mystery of the woman, and of the beast that carrieth her, which hath the seven heads and ten horns.

~ Revelation 17:7 (KJV)

The Word of God is truly perfect. The more we study it, the more amazing it becomes. We "marvel" at it. During Jesus' time on earth, people "marveled" at Him.

In today's 40/40, we see that, not only did the Israelites wander for forty years during the Exodus, but, in God's perfect epic story drama, there are forty chapters in the Book of Exodus!

In the parlance of stage performers, actors make an "exodus" as described by the term "Exit...stage left." It means marking the disappearance of a character from the stage in the normal manner.

But soon, the true Church will be asked by God to "exit stage right." We will be making a supernaturally inspired disappearance from the world's secular and apostate religious institutions.

*Then I heard another voice from heaven say: "Come out of her
MY PEOPLE, so that you will not share in her sins or contract
any of her plagues."*

~ Revelation 18:4 (Berean Study Bible)

Did you ever wonder what God's People are doing IN the Whore of
Babylon in the first place???

As we continue to study the ten commandments, we note the Second
Commandment given to the Israelites in the wilderness was:

*Thou shalt not make unto thee any graven image, or any
likeness of any thing that is in heaven above, or that is in the
earth beneath, or that is in the water under the earth.*

~Exodus 20:4 (KJV)

Why this strict prohibition against graven images? I believe it is because
when we "engraven" an image in our minds and/or fashion one with our
hands, we are not able to recognize when the real deal is in front of us.

When John first saw the Whore of Babylon in his apocalyptic vision, it
says he looked upon her with wonder. Let's examine this word in the Greek
(G2295 and G2296):

"a wonderful thing, a marvel"
"to be wondered at, to be had in admiration"

The Apostle John, the one closest to Jesus' bosom, would not look
with admiration upon a wicked whore! He would only "marvel" in
astonishment when he saw the image of what the Latter Day Church
had become! Perhaps at first, John thought this was something to be
desired...an image of worldly acceptance that he hoped the church would
eventually obtain.

During John's time the Church was hunted, persecuted, exiled, fed
to lions, and killed by Roman Government. Now through his "vision
glasses" he saw a "woman" who was the "belle of the ball"...dining with

kings, dressed in finery and actually "riding the beast"...*in lockstep with the governments themselves!* John was utterly amazed. How can this be? What a complete reversal!

Like John, we need to refocus. Our goal, as Christ's Bride, is not to prostitute ourselves with modern-day Roman governments. Based on the apostasy that is spreading like cancer throughout the churches of today, we need to drop our graven images of what we desire the church to look like. The True Church must begin to look more and more like the First Century Church and depart from the grotesque Babylonian image of Revelation.

So, COME OUT OF HER MY PEOPLE. Exit this apostasy. It may require a "forty day" trek through the desert first, but the Promised Land is up ahead.

Repentance Prayer:

Heavenly Father, It's time to leave behind my "sacred cows" and stop this idle idol worship. I begin at the beginning by making You the only Lord of my life. You are my Master and, at your side, I will enter into the Promised Land. Let me not fashion myself according to the ways of the world, nor even my pre-conceived notions but let me allow You to transform me into Your image. Teach me to listen to You and not seek the approbation or applause of the world systems. Help me to put aside my own disobedient ways and follow You without question. I pray this prayer in the Name above all names, the King of kings, the Lord of lords, Yeshua. ~ Amen

Scriptures to help me cleanse with His Word:

_____

_____

_____

DAY #17
Carved in Stone
His Name Written All Over It

40 Years of Peace for Israelites Under Judge Othniel

He who has an ear, let him hear what the Spirit says to the churches. To him who overcomes, I will give some of the hidden manna to eat. And I will give him a white stone, and on the stone a new name written which no one knows except him who receives it."

~ Revelation 2:17 (NKJV)

OTHNIEL. Now there's a bible name you don't hear very often. Othniel was the very first Judge of the twelve Judges of Israel. Today in our list of 40/40's we see that Othniel ruled for forty years and all forty years of his reign were years of peace for Israel. That alone should have given him a higher name recognition rating!

Today's we also examine commandment #3 of the ten commandments:

"Thou shalt not take the name of the Lord thy God in vain."
~Exodus 20:7 KJV

I think a very narrow understanding of this commandment is actually held today by the majority of Christians. If we took a poll, most people would say that it means they shouldn't swear using God's name. While that is most certainly true, there is so much more to this command than just gaining control over one's tongue.

Othniel, Caleb's brother, came on the scene when Israel was being oppressed by their Mesopotamian neighbors. He defeated them and conquered their town to be put into the hands of the Tribe of Judah. (Judges 3:9-11 NKJV). As a reward, Caleb (the hero from an earlier devotional) gave him his daughter as a bride. He also received her allotment of land from the Promised Land to carry on Caleb's line. All of this from a man who only gets a couple of lines in the Bible. However, no fifteen minutes of fame for this guy. He's permanently engraved in Holy Scripture for all of eternity!

Othniel shows us that God is all powerful and those who rely upon His Name are able to do memorable works. With God as our leader, an unknown "no name" can help save all of Israel and thus, share in the apportioning of the Promised Land. This should motivate all of us! Imagine if you or I were able to bring forty years of peace to our land!

That's why we shouldn't take God's Name in vain. Any mention of God's name contains His Holy Power. To throw it around in a fit of rage is a very serious sin. God's name should be a banner that goes before us and a rear protective guard behind us.

In Revelation, God says He will give a *new name* written on a white stone to those who will overcome. (Revelation 2:17 NKJV). I don't know about you, but that scripture always seemed a bit obscure to me. In modern times, when our name is written on a white stone, we are usually six feet under...not exactly something we generally get excited about!

Yet, white stone, while often representing a tomb in scripture, is reminiscent of the alabaster box of perfume smashed to pieces at the Savior's feet. When we hand in our temples of alabaster (this life), God promises to give us back so much more....to become part of His Heavenly household. We die to this life. Alabaster is a stone that smashes to dust, and to dust we shall return until Christ returns for us and makes us His Memorial throughout all eternity.

I don't know what will be written on each of our white stones. However, I know it will be eternal, and anything that we have done for the Lord won't be in vain.

Repentance Prayer:

Heavenly Father, I honor Your Holy Name. Please give me the courage of Othniel to carry out Your assignment under the banner of Your Holy Name. Deliver me from enemy strongholds. Help me to begin using the power of daily repentance to be an overcomer. I want to receive a white stone, a NEW NAME that only You can give. As a member of Your Royal Priesthood, help me become a godly servant like Othniel. As I repent, discipline me to increasingly reflect the character of Christ our High Priest, Yeshua, in whose Name we pray. ~ Amen

Scriptures to help me cleanse with His Word:

_____

_____

_____

DAY #18
Restraining Order
Side-Walk Prophet

40 Years of Rest after Deborah Inspired Israel to Victory

Submit yourselves, then, to God. Resist the devil, and he will flee from you. ~James 4:7 (NIV)

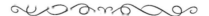

In today's devotional, following our 40/40's outline, we see that forty years of peace followed Deborah and Barak's victory. As with all characters in the Bible, Deborah and Barak represent something greater than themselves. I believe they are a representation of Christ and His Church. We restrain the devil by resisting him.

In order to win this battle, Christ does not demand us to accompany Him, but like Barak, He asks us to go. We must walk willingly by His side.

> *Barak said to her, "If you will go with me, I will go; but if you will not go with me, I will not go!"* ~ Judges 4:8 (ESV)

Deborah says "yes" but acknowledges that the victory credit would then go to a woman:

> *"I will certainly go with you," Deborah replied, "but the road you are taking will bring you no honor, because the LORD will be selling Sisera into the hand of a woman." So Deborah got up and went with Barak to Kedesh.*
> ~ Judges 4:9 (Berean Study Bible)

I don't think she said this in an arrogant way. I think she said it in this spirit: *"Are you sure you want me to come along? People will then say that the victory will be attributed to a woman."*

Barak still agrees and Jael, the Kenite woman, (not Deborah) ends up driving the final spike through Sisera's head, thereby defeating the king of the Canaanites.

In God's wry sense of humor, God always has the last laugh lest we think too highly of ourselves. The name "Jael" is actually comprised of two Hebrew Words:

> Jah = The shortened form of "Yahweh"
> El = shortened form of "Elohim"

Thus, GOD gets the double victory credit. This is truly "hilaros" (Greek #2431 Strong's Concordance) as the whole Bible drama is! When we walk in the Covenant at His side...the Two become One.

For today's highlighted Commandment, we acknowledge commandment #4:

> *"Remember the Sabbath day, to keep it holy"*
> *~Exodus 20:8 NKJV*

The Sabbath is a God-ordained rest. We must rest in God as He is our Provider, He fights our battles. I believe Deborah completely understood this rest principle. Resting does not mean "doing nothing," it means we understand that our trustful obedience is what God asks of us always. We rightly acknowledge during a Sabbath rest that we are under God's provision and God's rule so that we are always "battle ready."

So, will you go to battle with the Lord? If we follow the Commander-in-Chief into battle, He will, like the chivalrous Gentleman that He is, allow us to be honored.

But in the end, it's all done in His Name.

And the land was peaceful 40 years.
~ Judges 5:31(b) (Holman Christian Study Bible)

Repentance Prayer:

Heavenly Father, Teach me to fully grasp what an honor it is to serve You. So often I foolishly think that I am doing you a favor instead of understanding what an incredible opportunity it is to fight alongside You. Help me to comprehend what the principle of Sabbath rest really means as I rest within your Covenant and rest in the knowledge that You are always faithful. As I REPENT, discipline me to increasingly reflect Your character in the example of Christ our High Priest, in whose Name we pray. ~ Amen

Scriptures to help me cleanse with His Word:

_____

_____

_____

DAY #19
Out of Order
In the Lineup

40 Years Served by Judge Barak with Israelites

Let all things be done decently and in order.
~ 1 Corinthians 14:40 (NKJV)

In today's devotional, following our 40/40's outline, we continue studying the story of Deborah and Barak. There were forty years of peace following Deborah and Barak's victory but there is something else that is often overlooked.

Very few people realize that Deborah's counterpart, Barak, is mentioned again in the New Testament. Thus, it is appropriate to give him the recognition that he deserves.

We already know that Deborah was a judge from the scripture:

> *And Deborah, a prophetess, the wife of Lappidoth, she judged Israel <u>at that time.</u> And she dwelt under the palm tree of Deborah between Ramah and Bethel in mount Ephraim: and the children of Israel came up to her for judgment.*
> *~ Judges 4:4-5 (KJV)*

While Barak was not officially mentioned as a "Judge" in the Old Testament, his inclusion in the list of great Judges/Kings in Hebrews 11 removes all doubt of his status:

> *And what more shall I say? I do not have time to tell about Gideon, Barak, Samson and Jephthah, about David and Samuel and the prophets, who through faith conquered kingdoms, administered justice, and gained what was promised.*
>
> ~ Hebrews 11:32-33(a) (NIV)

Why wasn't Deborah, also a Judge, mentioned in this list?

Let's look more closely at the scriptural time line. Often, Deborah is given the credit as the female Judge of Israel during the forty year time period following the war with the Canaanites. However, based on the scripture in Hebrews 11, it is clear that Barak was the one ruling Israel during that time of peace.

Deborah was a Judge during the previous twenty years...a time that Israel was in disobedience and chaos/disorder. Let's look at the verse immediately preceding the one that mentions Deborah as a Judge of Israel:

> *And the children of Israel cried unto the LORD: for he had nine hundred chariots of iron; <u>and TWENTY YEARS he mightily oppressed the children of Israel.</u>*
>
> ~ Judges 4:3 (KJV, emphasis added)

Then comes verse #4:

> *And Deborah, a prophetess, the wife of Lapidoth, she judged Israel <u>at that time.</u>* ~ Judges 4:4 (KJV, emphasis added)

God is a God of order. Women rulers were a sign of chaos and disorder within the camp and Israel could not be enjoying forty years of peace while a female Judge was raised up to rule them.

Godly women know that in order to remain UNDER the covenant, they must remain IN the correct ruling order of God:

Christ/Man

Church/Woman

Family of God/Children

The family is a microcosm example of the order that must be found within the Church. This scripture tells us what happens to Israel when they are disobedient:

> *Youths oppress My people, and women rule over them.*
> ~ Isaiah 3:12 (a) (Berean Study Bible, emphasis added)

This fits in perfectly with our Commandment of the Day which is the fifth commandment:

> *Honour thy father and thy mother*
> (Exodus 20:12(a) KJV)

Let's give Deborah and Barak, our spiritual ancestral line, the correct honor in biblical history. While Deborah correctly acknowledged that Israel had a spiritual problem, she rightly called on Barak to handle it!

> *And she sent and called Barak the son of Abinoam out of Kedesh-Naphtali*
> ~ Judges 4:6(a) (KJV)

It's time for the men of God to step up. Women may call out disorder and chaos, but if we want to see the victory for God's people...we need the men to get back in line.

Repentance Prayer:

Heavenly Father, Teach me to know my place in the Kingdom of God. I REPENT of any chaos and disorder that I have committed and fostered within the Church. Forgive me for any way in which I have not honored my father and my mother. Help me to reflect the Heavenly order that you created. Remind me that the devil is the author of chaos and confusion but You, Holy God, are the One who set the planets in proper order and the stars in the sky.

As I repent, discipline me to increasingly reflect Your character in the example of Christ our High Priest who reigns over us. May we willingly submit to Your order and Lordship.~ Amen

Scriptures to help me cleanse with His Word:

_____

_____

_____

DAY #20
Less is More
Down for the Count

40 Years of Peace after Gideon's Conquest

But to the cowardly and unbelieving and abominable and murderers and sexually immoral and sorcerers and idolaters and all liars, their place will be in the lake that burns with fire and sulfur. This is the second death.
~ Revelation 21:8 (Berean Study Bible)

Sadly, after Deborah and Barak were raised up by God, we see the same old pattern repeated by the children of Israel:

And the children of Israel did evil in the sight of the LORD: and the LORD delivered them into the hand of Midian seven years.
~ Judges 6:1(KJV)

In our ongoing series of 40/40's, we come upon Gideon threshing wheat on the threshing floor. But first let's "set the stage" of the state of Israel at that time.

And so it was, <u>when Israel had sown,</u> that the Midianites came up... and destroyed the increase of the earth, till thou come unto Gaza, and <u>left no sustenance for Israel,</u>....
and they entered into the land <u>to destroy it</u>.....
<u>and the children of Israel cried unto the Lord</u>.
~Excerpts from Judges 6: 3-6 (KJV, emphasis added)

When Gideon was called into action, Israel was in dire straits. Gideon had to winnow grain in secret just so the Midianites would not steal every little bit of food and sustenance from them.

> *Gideon threshed wheat by the winepress, to hide it from the Midianites.* ~ Judges 6:11(b) (KJV)

Chapter 6 begins with Gideon winnowing the wheat from the chaff and then the winnowing continues in Chapter 7 as God winnows Gideon's army.

In this chapter God winnowed down a fighting force from 32,000 to just three hundred, who were already badly outnumbered by an enemy of 120,000! (Judges 7:7 NKJV). Interestingly, those who were "afraid and trembling" were the first asked to leave. Cowards go to the lake of fire first in Revelation also (Revelation 21:8 NKJV). 22,000 departed leaving Gideon with just 10,000 now to fight 120,000...outnumbered 12 to 1.

I'm sure we would all be thinking: *OK God...you can stop now!* But God says..."You still have too many!" *Gulp.* "Yes," says God..."let's see who gulps."

> *The people are still too many; bring them down to the water and I will test them for you there.* ~ Judges 7:4 (NKJV)

God then knocked off another 9,700 men with only three hundred remaining who "lapped like dogs."

Why did God do this? I believe there are two reasons:

1) God winnows so we don't think that we save ourselves. *"Lest Israel vault themselves against Me saying mine own hand hath saved me.~* Judges 7:2(b) (KJV)
2) God wants us to develop faith. He only needs 1 person to make 1,000 flee and 2 people to make 10,000 flee. (Deuteronomy 32:30 NKJV). It's never been about "numbers" with God.

In today's devotional, we have also reached the sixth commandment for discussion.

"Thou Shalt Not Kill."

(Exodus 20:13 KJV)

Hmmm...Seriously, God? The entire three chapters on Gideon in Judges 6-8 are about his warlike destruction of the enemy and today You want to also address the sixth commandment?

Well, marching onward with the belief that God knows exactly what He is doing, let's continue studying.

While this commandment is most often stated as Thou Shalt Not "Kill," the correct word in the Hebrew is "ratsach" which refers to murder or homicide. No one would claim that a police officer "murdered" a school shooter or a terrorist. No one would say that a soldier "murdered" the enemy forces. No one would assert that a man committed a "homicide" on an armed thug intent on harming his family. There is a right use of force which is recognized by all societies.

Therefore when atheists claim that the God of the Old Testament is a "genocidal maniac" or some other such nonsense, it just doesn't ring true. Gideon saved his people from destruction by cutting down the enemy. The name "Gideon" literally means "hewer" or "cutter down." His fight against the Midianites was righteous in order to save the lives of his people.

God is doing the same thing today. He is separating the wheat from the chaff, the sheep from the goats, and the servant dog-like lappers from the greedy guzzlers. He needs to do another great work and it can only be done *with the few not the many.*

So the land had rest for forty years in the days of Gideon.
~Judges 8:28(b) (Berean Study Bible)

Repentance Prayer:

Heavenly Father, We acknowledge that this is going to be a time marked by great winnowing, trembling, quivering and shaking. Everything that can be shaken will be shaken so that what cannot be shaken remains.

We acknowledge that this is not going to be a pleasant time for the world. Yet, this is Your "Harvest Time." We celebrate Your separation of the kernel/meat from the chaff.

Like the Harvest Times of Israel, we look forward to the barley harvest which comes just before the wheat harvest. Both are brought about by the Latter Rains of Your Holy Spirit. Just as Barley was sifted by throwing it in the air and letting the wind (Holy Spirit) separate the kernel from the chaff, we know that Barley represents those with a soft heart towards repentance. Help us to be easily separated from the world as those who readily submit to your sifting process and be the first to REPENT.

As we enter Your Wheat Harvest, remove those of us who are planted and surrounded with the "tares." Let us not be resistant to "coming out" from the world. We acknowledge that this will require more shaking, trembling and quivering.

As Your Grape Harvest begins, help us understand the Mercy of Your Judgment which creates Spirit filled Wine: more passionate followers produced by Your Holy Judgment.

Help us to be prepared for the Olive Harvest. This will be even more intense. We will be sorely pressed on all sides but we rejoice in an increase in prophetic understanding. Some of us will need multiple pressings, creating Extra-Virgin lamp oil.

Your chosen Figs will then ripen. Your ripe Figs represent Churches and Leaders. May we be examples of "early figs." Churches must ripen or be cursed just as Jesus cursed the unproductive fig tree. The ripe ones will go on to bear much fruit. The others will shrivel and die in their apostasy.

Help us to prepare our hearts for the final stage of the separation of the sheep from the goats: War, persecution, martyrdom and bloodshed. We know this will be Your final merciful attempt to bring all nations to repentance.

As I personally repent, teach me to be like Gideon, though lowly, a great warrior through Your Power. ~Amen

Scriptures to help me cleanse with His Word:

_____

_____

_____

DAY #21
Sticks and Stones
The Harder They Fall

40 Days the Philistine Goliath taunted Israel

Yea, all kings shall fall down before him: all nations shall serve Him.

~ Psalm 72:11 (KJV)

For today's devotional we acknowledge the seventh commandment:

"Thou Shalt Not Commit Adultery"
(Exodus 20:14 KJV)

Everyone understands what adultery is within a marriage but what is spiritual adultery? Throughout the Bible God portrays His relationship with His people in marriage covenant terms. He expresses grief when they ignore Him and jealousy when they run to other false gods.

We commit spiritual adultery when we place anything in higher standing than our relationship with God. Are you breaking the Seventh Commandment?

Take this short test. Honestly is paramount or the results will be skewed. Consider each question carefully before you write down your answer:

#1) What/Who do you **THINK** about most often?

_____

#2) What/Who do you **TALK** about most often?

_____

#3) What/Who do you give your free **TIME** to the most often?

_____

#4) What do you spend your extra **TREASURE** (money) on most often?

_____

#5) Who do you turn to and **TRUST** the most when things get difficult?

_____

Now add up your responses. You will have found your God (or gods).

_____

If you answered honestly, many of you will end up with answers such as "Family" or "Friends" or even "Sports/Entertainment." The saddest Truth of all is most people will have to truthfully answer: "ME." I'm working on this also. He is Present to help us repent.

In our continuing devotional series on the "40/40's" we come across the story of David and Goliath. Goliath taunted the Israelites for forty days. King Saul offered up his daughter and riches to anyone who could defeat Goliath:

> Now the men of Israel had been saying, "Do you see this man who keeps coming out to defy Israel? To the man who kills him the king will give great riches. And he will give him his

daughter in marriage and exempt his father's house from taxation in Israel." ~1 Samuel 17:25 (Berean Study Bible)

But, I don't think David was interested in the "free goodies"...so he asked the question again!

> *David said to the men who stood by him, "What shall be done for the man who kills this Philistine, and takes away the reproach from Israel? For who is this uncircumcised Philistine that he should defy the armies of the living God?"* <u>*The people answered him in the same way,*</u> *"So shall it be done for the man who kills him."*   ~ 1 Samuel 17:26-27 (ESV)

We can almost see the wheels of David's mind working here. If I might be so bold as to attempt an example of his thoughts:

"That's NOT what I asked! What must be DONE to remove this OUTRAGE (sin) from God's people?"

It was a prophetic statement foreshadowing Christ. Nothing besides slaying the giant and honoring God was important to David.

David's heart was not adulterous towards God. No amount of free stuff offered by King Saul was what motivated him. He was motivated by righteous anger that this "uncircumcised Philistine" would dare defy and mock God by being allowed to remain standing for so long. Every moment (forty full days) that Goliath stood mocking the Israelites was one more day that Satan was laughing at the *lack of faith* among the Israelite army.

Interestingly, even after David volunteered, the Israelites continued to offer solutions to him which just weighed him down. He eschewed the armor of Saul, as we should shrug off man-made solutions to spiritual problems. Instead he rightly acknowledged that the same God who saved him from the clutches of the lion and the bear would also save him from this roaring beast.

His weapon of choice? A slingshot with 5 smooth stones.

In this one chapter we see that David **THOUGHT** about God, **TALKED** about God, offered his **TIME** to God, eschewed **TREASURE** for God and **TRUSTED** in God alone. He had all 5 stones in his sling...but when a person has this right attitude in their heart, God takes the devil down with One Solid Rock.

Repentance Prayer:

Heavenly Father, I repent. Please make me aware of any forms of spiritual adultery. Help me remove old sin patterns that attempt to filter You out of Your rightful position as first and foremost in my life. I receive Your rightful chastening because Your Holy Word says those whom You love you discipline. I turn to You now in trust and You alone I declare as Lord of my life. Help me to fall on my knees in repentance as I think about You, talk about You, offer my time and treasure to You and trust in You alone. ~ Amen

Scriptures to help me cleanse with His Word:

_____

_____

_____

DAY #22
Bringing Down The House
Warning: Strong Language

40 Years of Bondage to the Philistines
before Samson was Born

*And the rain came down, and the torrents came, and the
winds blew and beat upon that house; and it did not fall, for
its foundation had been lain upon the rock.*
~ Matthew 7:25 (Berean Literal Bible)

The story of Samson always amazes me. In our continuing series of the
40/40's, we see the familiar pattern of the nation of Israel once again:

*Again the children of Israel did evil in the sight of the LORD,
and the LORD delivered them into the hand of the Philistines
for forty years.*   ~ Judges 13:1 (NKJV)

At this point, in this epic biblical drama, one might be tempted to say:
*"What is wrong with these people? HOW many times do they have to go into
bondage before they learn their lesson?"*

It's so easy to not see *ourselves* in the story of the Israelites. Of course, We
would never do that, right? Hmmm…

Today's highlighted commandment is the eighth commandment:

"Thou shalt not steal."

(Exodus 20:15 KJV)

As we have been doing, we want to delve deeper into the meaning of the commandments as, hopefully, everyone already knows that it is sinful to take someone else's property. How are we "spiritually stealing" and how can we repent?

The story of Samson is perfect to illustrate the concept of spiritual stealing.

Do you want your entire life to be justified? There's only one way, Church...Get down on your knees and REPENT! Otherwise, your life and my life will amount to naught. We need to think of Christ's "justification" in terms of a bank account. We will all get to the end of life short. Those who put their trust in Christ will be "reconciled," just like a checkbook. In order for our account to be reconciled, it needs the approval of the Heavenly Bank CEO.

In scripture, many people started out as a big mess. BUT...what was the important difference? They persevered, they persisted. Then their lives became "justifiable." The name "Israel" was given to Jacob after he wrestled with the theophany of Christ. The very name "Israel" means "wrestled with God and perseveres." "He who perseveres and persists."

> Then the man said, *"Your name will no longer be Jacob, but Israel, because you have struggled with God and with humans and have overcome."*
> Jacob said, *"Please tell me your name."*
> But he replied, *"Why do you ask my name?"* Then he blessed him there.
> ~ Genesis 32: 28-29 (NIV, emphasis added)

Amazingly, this is the same story as Samson's father Manoah in Judges!

> *And Manoah (Samson's father) said unto the angel of the*
> *LORD, <u>What is thy name</u>, that when thy sayings come to pass*
> *we may do thee honour?*
> *And the angel of the LORD said unto him, <u>Why askest*
> *thou thus after my name</u>, seeing it is secret?*
> ~Judges 13: 17-18 (KJV, emphasis added)

In some other versions of scripture translation, we see this word "secret" (for God's Name) meaning *wonderful, incomprehensible, extraordinary.* Thus, the Theophanic Angel knew that His Name could not fully be understood yet.

"Why do you ask My Name?" In both stories, I humbly believe Jacob and Manoah were really asking the same question:

> *"To Whom may we give the credit?"*

We are to take our entire life and lay it down on the altar as a "living sacrifice," (Romans 12:1 NKJV) otherwise we are stealing from God. All things are done for Him, through Him and to Him, but...let's not steal God's Glory. All glory goes to God.

> *Then Samson called out to the LORD: "O Lord GOD, please*
> *remember me. Strengthen me, O God, just once more, so that*
> *with one vengeful blow I may pay back the Philistines for my*
> *two eyes."*
> ~ Judges 16:28 (Bercan Study Bible, emphasis added)

Samson is a shadow-type of Christ. Christ redeems His "two eyes," His two lampstands...Christians and Jews. The only way we can be saved is if Christ pays for us.

If we don't relate to the Jewish story, we are not understanding the entire plot...If *they* don't make it out alive, we don't make it out alive. If the Bible drama was a movie, we should all be on the edge of our seats right now when we finally realize "Who dunnit?"

WE are the whiny complainers in the desert...

WE are the adulterous idol worshipers...

WE are the fickle, feckless, fallible nation of sinners...

We must look onward with great anticipation to see the Jews (and ourselves!) rescued by Super-Samson Christ. So...let's not try to steal the show. Yeshua's Name must be highlighted in the final credits!

<u>Repentance Prayer:</u>

Heavenly Father, Please forgive me for stealing from You spiritually. I REPENT for the ways I have been filled with my own pride and have spiritually robbed glory that is only due to You. I repent for not submitting to You fully. Bring down this "house" of pride and self-idol worship. Help me to accept the "strong language" of Your Holy Word and apply it to myself first so that I can assist others to repent also. When asked of me to Whom I give credit for transformation in my life, let Your Holy Name, the Name of Yeshua, be readily on my lips. ~ Amen

Scriptures to help me cleanse with His Word:

_____

_____

_____

DAY #23
No Guts, No Glory
Lights Out

40 Years Eli Judged Israel before the Glory
of the Lord Departed (Ichabod)

*Remember therefore from where you have fallen: repent and do
the first works, or else I will come to you quickly and remove
your lampstand from its place-unless you repent.*
~ Revelation 2:5 (NKJV)

For today's 40/40 we see that Eli was a Judge of Israel for a total of forty years. The story of Eli and his evil sons is a long and interesting one which cannot be fully covered in our short devotional series. We encourage you to spend some time reading these 4 chapters (1 Samuel, Chapters 1-4) for a complete account of this very relevant biblical story.

For today, we will simply concentrate on the term "Ichabod." When God was speaking to little Samuel, it was just before "lights out" in the Temple:

> *and before the lamp of God went out in the tabernacle of the
> Lord where the ark of God was, and while Samuel was lying
> down* ~ 1 Samuel 3:3 (NKJV)

Also, today's highlighted commandment is the ninth commandment:

> *"Thou shalt not bear false witness against thy neighbor."*
> Exodus 20:16 KJV

Pastor Jeffrey Daly

When Eli was instructing Samuel on how to "hear from God," Eli insisted that Samuel tell him the Truth, the whole Truth and nothing but the Truth. Eli, as a high priest, knew that nothing but the full Truth would be helpful. Little Samuel (interestingly, a name that means "heard God") was, at first, very reticent to tell Eli the harsh message of Judgment he had just received.

> And Samuel feared to shew Eli the vision.
> ~ 1 Samuel 3:15(b) (KJV)

Nevertheless, at Eli's insistence, Samuel tells him that God's judgment will fall on Eli and his sons and there is nothing that Eli can do to change that fact.

After hearing Samuel's vision, Eli resigned himself to God's Judgment.

> So Samuel told him everything and hid nothing from him. And he said, "It is the LORD; let Him do what seems good to Him."
> ~1 Samuel 3:18 (NASB)

Now why is this important and how is it relevant to our message today? We see Eli's sons taking the best prime cuts of the altar sacrifice, and sleeping with prostitutes in the Temple. Eli, as the High Priest, needed to not only tell them the Truth (which Eli did)...but, to also *restrain* them from doing this evil.

The Lord told Samuel:

> For I have told him that I will judge his house forever for the iniquity which he <u>knoweth</u>; because his sons made themselves vile, and he <u>restrained them not</u>.
> ~ 1 Samuel 3:13 (KJV, emphasis added)

So Eli knew the Truth but refused to act on it. Eli was "bearing a false witness" by his inactivity. Faith demands action. Inaction is the ultimate sign of no faith.

The church today can preach and teach until His Kingdom come, but if there is no restraint of sin, God's judgment will fall. It's not enough to simply say *"This is sinful"* without any restraint in the church body.

Today we repent of spiritually bearing false witness and breaking the ninth commandment. There are many "ear ticklers" who want to ignore the corruption in the churches today. (2 Timothy 4:3 NASB). They bear a false witness by a false prophecy of "everything is going to be alright" and "nothing to see here, folks, just move along."

Instead of having their ears "tickled," God says He is going to send a Judgment so profound that all ears will *tingle* (1 Samuel 3:11 NKJV).

When God enacted His Judgment on the House of Eli, Eli's apostate sons were slain on the same day in battle. Eli, upon hearing the news, fell back, broke his neck and died. Eli's pregnant daughter-in-law was so burdened that she immediately went into labor. As she was dying, she delivered a son and named him "Ichabod" which means "the glory of the Lord has departed." (1 Samuel 4:21 NKJV).

The Hebrew language is very descriptive and sometimes it even sounds wryly humorous. "Ichabod" sounds a lot like "Icky Body." That's exactly what we have when the glory of God departs the Temple.

Let's repent. We need to get rid of the "Icky Body" and submit to Christ as He prepares us as His Bride without spot or wrinkle. (Ephesians 5:27 ESV).

Repentance Prayer:

Heavenly Father, Please forgive me for bearing false witness through my inactivity in restraining evil. I REPENT for the ways I have given an "ear tickling" message instead of an "ear tingling" message. Moving onward, please fill me with boldness to tell the Truth, the whole Truth and nothing but the Truth, so help me Jesus Christ. Lord Jesus, You are the Way, the Truth and the Life. I repent for not submitting to You fully. Help me to accept the message of Judgment for sin in Your Holy Word and apply it to myself first so that I can assist others in repenting also. I pray this prayer in the Name above all names, the King of kings, the Lord of lords, YESHUA. ~ Amen

Scriptures to help me cleanse with His Word:

_____

_____

_____

DAY #24
The Walking Wounded
Well-Healed

40 Stripes = The Maximum Punishment
for the Wicked Man

He was wounded for our transgressions, he was bruised for our iniquities: the chastisement of our peace was upon him; and with his stripes we are healed. ~ Isaiah 53:5 (KJV)

In our continuing series of the biblical 40/40's we note the Old Testament punishment of forty lashes.

How many lashes did Jesus receive? People often answer "forty lashes" but the scripture is actually silent on this. Many people believe it is only 39 lashes because of this Old Testament law:

He may receive no more than forty lashes, lest your brother be beaten any more than that and be degraded in your sight. ~ Deuteronomy 25:3 (Berean Study Bible)

I'm going to suggest that our Lord and Savior Yeshua received more than 40 lashes. There was no reason for the Roman government to follow any Jewish customs in the punishment of their prisoners. Some theologians reason that the Romans would not give too many lashes so the condemned person would still be able to carry their own cross.

However, as we know from scripture, Simon the Cyrene was conscripted to carry Christ's cross the rest of the way to Golgotha (Matthew 27:32 NKJV). Therefore, it is reasonable to conclude that our Lord was whipped far beyond what most prisoners can physically endure.

Interestingly, the name Simon the Cyrene, when understood etymologically, means: "He who hears and thus has higher authority or standing." We can say that Simon was promoted in that day of his public humiliation.

National repentance in days past was called "days of public humiliation." I believe we have lost something in the translation now that we no longer use that word. "Humiliation" has taken on negative undertones instead of a required status for all Christians.

Today we don't see a lot of public humiliation. We mostly see politicians and celebrities boasting and talking themselves up.

Our focus today is the final Commandment, the tenth commandment:

> *"Thou Shalt Not Covet."*
> ~Exodus 20:17 (KJV)

How do we spiritually covet? We covet when we seek God's Glory but we don't also seek to share in His humiliation.

> *And that servant who knew his master's will, and <u>did not prepare himself</u> or do according to his will, shall be beaten with many STRIPES. But he who did not know, yet committed things deserving of stripes, shall be beaten with few. For everyone to whom much is given, from him much will be required; and to whom much has been committed, of him they will ask the more.*
> ~Luke 12:47-48 (NKJV, emphasis added)

Christ, the Supreme Judge, is returning in fiery Judgment to rule righteously. The very next verse says this:

> *I have come to ignite a fire on the earth, and how I wish it were*
> *already kindled!* ~ Luke 12:49 (Berean Study Bible)

Jesus is confirming that He is coming with Judgment fire, but He PREFERS if we judge ourselves beforehand and that this fire is already <u>kindled upon his return</u>. We need to keep the home fire hearths of our hearts burning for His return.

This is why individual and national repentance is so important. Those who want to reign with Christ must be "the walking wounded." Those who are repentant are wounded, they are burdened in their hearts...not only of their own sin but of the sins of their nation.

In the ancient world, royalty was signified by the color purple. When the soldiers mocked Jesus Christ, they put a purple robe on Him which actually confirmed His Kingship:

> *Therefore Jesus went forth outside, wearing the thorny crown*
> *and the purple robe. And he says to them, "Behold the man!"*
> ~ John 19:5 (Berean Literal Bible)

Purple dye was the most expensive variety known in the first century. It was afforded only to those of noble or royal birth and high-level officials. Purple is also the color of a bruise.

It seems fitting that in modern time, those who are wounded while serving, receive a special purple recognition. Prepare yourself Church. If we want to wear purple royal robes with Christ...first we need a bruised Purple Heart.

Repentance Prayer:

Heavenly Father, Please forgive me for coveting Your Glory without also bearing Your burden. I repent for the ways I have failed to humiliate myself before You. Moving onward, please fill my heart with humility as I acknowledge my own sins and assist others with repenting of theirs. Prepare me to overcome trials and tribulations so that I might persevere until You rule and reign. I repent for not submitting to You fully. Help me to carry Your cross and receive the highest honor possible to hear my Master say "Well done" as I enter into Your Eternal Joy. ~ Amen

Scriptures to help me cleanse with His Word:

_____

_____

_____

DAY #25
Eye Opener
Lens Cleaning

40 Days Elijah's Strength Lasted after Food from Angels

Behold, the eye of the LORD is on those who fear him, on those who hope in his steadfast love ~ Psalm 33:18 (ESV)

In our previous devotionals we reviewed:

~ The 7 Things the Lord Hates
~ The 7 Deadly Sins
~ The 10 Commandments

Next we, at National Day of Repentance, have long felt God calling us to lovingly expose counterfeit spirituality within the Church.

In our continuing study of the "40/40's" in scripture, we come upon Elijah continuing in strength for forty days and forty nights after being fed by angels.

> *A second time the angel of the LORD returned and touched him, saying, "Get up and eat, or the journey will be too much for you. So he got up and ate and drank. And strengthened by that food, he walked <u>forty days and forty nights</u> until he reached Horeb, the mountain of God.*
> ~ 1 Kings 19:7-8 (Berean Study Bible, emphasis added)

If we want to be fortified spiritually, we need to make sure we are eating healthy spiritual food that only comes from a heavenly source...Angel food instead of devil food cake!

Experts tell us that the best way to spot a counterfeit is to become intimately familiar with the original. With God's help, this will be our objective: to assist us in becoming more intimate with Christ so that all other false practices will be removed from the Bride who is to be presented without spot or wrinkle.

To begin, we must start at the beginning: GOD. God is the Original, the True One of Inestimable Value. Then, we must grasp how Satan operates. Most people would state that Satan is the opposite of God. While he does oppose God, he does so by being subtle and crafty. He sidles up to the Original and creates a counterfeit. His methods are not obvious at first, just as a snake in the grass is not easily noticeable.

We pray that even if you have been "bit" by these counterfeit spiritual practices, these next 12 Devotionals will be spiritual "anti-venom." We pray, like Paul, you will be able to simply "shake it off," removing false beliefs through time spent with the Lord repenting.

But Paul shook the creature off into the fire and suffered no ill effects. ~ Acts 28:5 (Berean Study Bible)

As God is a God of order, we will continue to present this information in an orderly fashion. The Body of Christ will be our "presentation chart" from top to bottom. Today we begin with the EYES since the very word "occult" is related to the eyes (e.g. ocular) and literally means "seeing." The eyes are the window to the soul.

> *Your eye is the lamp of your body. When your vision is clear,*
> *your whole body also is full of light. But when it is poor, your*
> *body is full of darkness.* ~ Luke 11:34 (Berean Study Bible)

The "All-Seeing Eye" is often associated with those who are involved in evil occult practices. Whether you scoff at the overuse of the term

"Illuminati" or not, there is an important spiritual Truth here. What "enlightens" you? Remember, Lucifer was an "angel of light."

As little children, many of us sang the Sunday School song:

> *"Be careful little eyes what you see, be careful little eyes what you see, for the Lord up above is looking down in love, so be careful little eyes what you see."*

Those who have an awareness that God is watching them, *behave* like Holy God is watching them! Those who want to keep sinning, turn away from this awareness.

> *Everyone who does evil hates the Light, and does not come into the Light for fear that his deeds will be exposed.*
> ~ John 3:20 (Berean Study Bible)

The further and further we move away from God in our countries, and in our personal lives, the more we will "see" (pardon the pun), "Big Brother" governmental intrusion of demonic watching.

We need to acknowledge God is our Provider. It does not come from government programs that demand loyalty, accountability and ungodly secularism.

Judgment begins in the House of the Lord, so it is not surprising that we will see purification occur here first. Godly watchmen need to keep watching with clear eyes based on scriptural Truth. It's time to put in the Heavenly eye drops:

> *I counsel you to buy from Me...eye-salve to anoint your eyes so that you may see.* ~ Revelation 3:18 (Berean Literal Bible)

Repentance Prayer:

Heavenly Father, Please forgive me for the times I knowingly or unknowingly participated in counterfeit spiritual activities. I

REPENT for the ways in which I have desired spiritual power in an ungodly manner. Moving onward help me to see the schemes of the devil. Prepare me for battle using Your Power and equipped with the armor of God. Heal my blindness and open my eyes to the correct spiritual perspective. Help me to trust in You as my Provider and not temporal governments. I pray this prayer in the Name above all names, the King of kings, the Lord of lords, YESHUA who restores my sight. ~ Amen

Scriptures to help me cleanse with His Word:

DAY #26
Uncharted Waters
Running on Empty?

40 Camels Sent to Elisha to Enquire
if King Would Recover

He who believes in Me, as the Scripture has said, out of his
heart will flow rivers of living water. ~ John 7:38 (NKJV)

Sadly, a New Age spirit has invaded many church activities. A simple scroll through Church websites will show such topics as: "Christian Yoga," "Breath Prayer," "Mindfulness," "At-One-Ment," "Contemplative Prayer," "Prayer Soaking" and many other adulterated attempts at mixing godly principles with the devil's counterfeit.

This is a tough topic. I bet at this point we have managed to offend about 50% of our readership. We've absorbed so much of this falsity that we have not paused enough to do a "spirit check" before considering what we are putting into our minds.

In our ongoing series of the "40/40's" found in scripture, we come upon the King of Syria inquiring of Elisha. Along with the king's servant, he sent Elisha 40 camels burdened with an offering (2 Kings 8:9 NKJV). The camels represented the extent of his anguish regarding his sole question:

"Will I recover?"
~ 2 Kings 8:9(b) (Berean Study Bible)

I'm sure an entire book can be written on this topic but for today's devotional we have to cut right to the core of the issue. All the occult methodologies mentioned above require one thing: SELF FOCUS. Even if they sound really nice, such as saying a few words from scripture over and over again, this violates Christ's admonition to not be repetitious like pagan practices.

> And when you pray, do not use vain repetitions as the heathen
> do. For they think that they will be heard for their many words.
> ~ Matthew 6:7 (NKJV)

The devil is sneaky and crafty. If he can convince us that mind-numbing repetition or inward focus is OK, as long as we throw in a few scripture verses, he is more than happy to deceive in that manner. Remember, the devil quoted scripture when trying to tempt Christ in the wilderness.

Sadly, the King of Syria did not recover and he was eventually overthrown and replaced by his own household servant. The Syrians continue to be a thorn in Israel's side to this very day. We can be burdened, like the King of Syria, but if we don't start practicing Godly behaviors, we will not recover.

Jews in both ancient and modern Judaism ritually purify themselves in a mikveh. What few modern people realize about a proper mikveh is that it must have a source of running (aka *living*) water. It is not like a bathtub for soaking but an ever-moving stream.

Demonic meditative methodologies, which flow inward but not outward symbolize stagnation. It is a dead inner focus instead of an alive and moving one. God's Holy Spirit flows *through* us. We are not to attempt to "soak" Him in selfishly. In trying to "fill" ourselves, we instead will find ourselves unclean.

There is an authentic spiritual equivalent to this counterfeit spirituality. When we enter into relationship with Christ, we drink in His Living Water. Jesus asked the servants at the wedding of Cana to fill all the empty vessels with water and then He turned them into spirit filled wine.

But whoever drinks the water I give him will never thirst.
Indeed the water I give him will become in him a fount of water
springing up to eternal life.

~ John 4:14 (Berean Study Bible)

So, as God's chosen vessels, we need to understand that we are already filled and set our minds on things above instead of emptying them with things of the world.

Allow your mind to be filled with God's Holy Word and watch the Spirit begin to flow.

Repentance Prayer:

Heavenly Father, Please forgive me for the times I knowingly or unknowingly participated in counterfeit spiritual activities. I REPENT for the ways in which I have desired spiritual power in an ungodly manner. Moving onward help me to see the schemes of the devil. Prepare me for battle using Your Power and equipped with the armor of God. Fill my mind with Living Water and heal me spiritually from head to toe as I submit to Your ways and not the ways of the kingdom of darkness. Moving onward, teach me to submit to the Head of the Body of Christ, our Lord and Savior, Yeshua. We pray this prayer in Yeshua's Holy Name. ~ Amen

Scriptures to help me cleanse with His Word:

_____

_____

_____

DAY #27
Mouthing Off
The Best Laid Plans

40 Years of King Jehoash's Reign

A man's heart plans his course, but the LORD determines his steps. ~Proverbs 16:9 (Berean Study Bible)

Today in our "Body of Christ chart" we focus on our mouth. The Lord has been laying something on my heart lately. There are words that we need to use sparingly, or not at all, in our vocabulary when speaking of our labor for the Lord:

Plan, Scheme, Method, Strategize, Craft, Tactic, Game Plan, Plot, Maneuver, Stratagem, Ambition, Blueprint, Formula, Devise, Concoct, Formulate (and I'm sure there are many more synonyms).

In order to be clear and not legalistic, some of these words can be sincerely used in their proper context. However, we need to acknowledge that when we are laboring in love towards advancing God's Kingdom onward, He already has His Divine Sovereign Plan in place. He is the Commander-in-Chief and we are the foot soldiers obeying His orders.

For today's continuing series of the "40/40's" in scripture, we come across the forty years of rule by King Jehoash. King Jehoash (sometimes also spelled Joash) ruled righteously as long as his righteous uncle, High Priest Jehoiada, was alive (2 Kings 12:2 NKJV). However, after Jehoiada died, King Jehoash, became involved with some very evil strategists. Speaking death, Jehoash gave the command to stone the new high priest, Jehoiada's son. His reign ended poorly, reintroducing idol worship to Israel.

If we find ourselves being tempted to use any of these words, we should phrase it like this:

I'm PLANNING on finishing this project later this evening...GOD WILLING.

Here is what God's Holy Word says on the matter:

> *Come now, you who say, "Today or tomorrow we will go to such and such a city, spend a year there, buy and sell, and make a profit;" whereas you do not know what will happen tomorrow. For what is your life? It is even a vapor that appears for a little time and then vanishes away. Instead you ought to say, "If the Lord wills, we shall live and do this or that." But now you boast in your arrogance. All such boasting is evil.*
> ~ James 4:13-16 (NKJV, emphasis added)

Despite what popularity pulpits like to ramble on about, mankind does not have goodwill without Christ. The only good within us is by the indwelling of the Holy Spirit. Otherwise, the heart is wicked and deceitful beyond measure.

> *Many are the plans in a person's heart, but it is the Lord's purpose that prevails.* ~ Proverbs 19:21 (NIV)

We dare not attempt to mess with the goodwill of His Holy Work...just as employees can do nothing worse than bring dishonor to the years of goodwill built up at a successful company. We need to tread cautiously here as we are walking on Holy Ground. Once the goodwill of an organization is damaged, it is often difficult to get it back.

Therefore, the only "plan" we should have is to advance the Kingdom of Light onward with the goodwill that already exists from the foundation that Christ has already laid.

Let's not be so hasty as to ignore two thousand years of Christ's Sovereign Plan in favor of man's strategies. Our "game plan" is the Holy Word of God, our "advertisement" is the Holy Spirit and our "Chief Operating Officer" is Father God.

Our only "strategy" should be taking more ground for the Kingdom through the Peace of God that comes from encouraging others to lay down their arms in repentance.

Repentance Prayer:

Heavenly Father, Please forgive me for the times I thought that I was in charge instead of following Your pre-ordained Plan. I REPENT for the ways in which I have attempted to strategize and plot in a spiritually ungodly manner. Moving onward help me to see that manipulation is a scheme of the devil. Prepare me for battle using Your Power, equipped with the armor of God and following Your battle plan. Fill my mind with humility to obey You and submit to Your authority in all things. I pray this prayer in the Name above all names, the King of kings, the Lord of lords, YESHUA. ~ Amen

Scriptures to help me cleanse with His Word:

_____

_____

_____

DAY #28
Hand It Over
Come Out In the Wash

40 "by the space of" God gave Israel King Saul

Do not be anxious about anything, but in everything by prayer and supplication with thanksgiving let your requests be made known to God. ~ Philippians 4:6 (ESV)

Be careful little hands what you do. Be careful little hands what you do. For the Lord up above is looking down in love, so be careful little hands what you do.
~ Childhood Sunday School Song.

Today, we focus again on the Body of Christ and our HANDS. A popular Facebook "prayer" emoji shows two hands pointed upwards. While I realize, most people do not give this much thought, this image is actually the Hindu Namaste sign. You will see this gesture repeated in worldly Hollywood awards shows as they honor each other for their secular works. It literally means: "I bow to the god in you."

Very few people also recognize that "prayer beads" are a consistent tradition in NON-Biblical thought and practice:

In Islam known as = Misbaha
In Hindusim known as = Japamala
In Buddhism/Sihkism known as = Malas or Seik Badi
In Baha'i known as = Prayer Beads

Pastor Jeffrey Daly

In Native American Indian worship known as = Spirit Beads
In Chinese Mysticism known as = Baoding Balls (Yin/Yang)
In Wicca/Paganism known as = Witch's Beads
In Eastern Orthodox known as = Prayer Rope
In Roman Catholicism known as = Rosary Beads

These are all derived from "worry beads" originating in Greek and secular culture. Also known as *"begleri"* they were used to pass the time or keep the hands busy.

Now, as scripture clearly tells us, faith without works is dead, however, these practices are not works but something entirely different. They are more in the realm of obsessive compulsion disorders believing that if you DO or DON'T do them, something good or bad will happen. This is superstition and their use cannot be found anywhere in scripture not even symbolically.

It reminds me of the humorous definition of "worrying:" It's like a rocking chair. It gives you something to do but never gets you anywhere.

Interestingly, while doing the research for our 40/40's series, I was surprised to find there is some biblical controversy over how long Saul reigned in Israel. Without going into superfluous detail, the Old Testament scripture is unclear on whether Saul was forty years old and/or reigned for forty years as king. Perhaps he was a true "40/40" both facts possibly being true! I urge you to study up on this yourself for some amazing textual history. The KJV in the New Testament continues with the mystery in its vague wording:

> And afterward they desired a king: and God gave unto them
> Saul the son of Cis, a man of the tribe of Benjamin, <u>by the space
> of forty years</u>.   ~ Acts 13:21 (KJV, emphasis added)

Yet, Old Testament translations range from 2 - 42 years!

Note this explanation from KJV Today:

> "*The footnotes to most translations (ESV, NIV, NASB) at 1 Samuel 13:1 say that the Hebrew text is missing the number of the years of Saul's age and reign. The Septuagint curiously omits the verse.*"

As I am one who believes there are no "accidents" with Sovereign God, maybe we should just accept this as a holy metaphor. We don't definitively know how old he was upon taking the throne, nor how long he reigned perhaps because he was the king who served prior to the Throne of David. As such, I believe he symbolizes the earthly kings who will rule over us prior to Christ's return.

How long will we have to wait for Messiah to take his rightful place on the Throne? Even Jesus Christ, when he walked on Earth, said He did not know. Since Jesus is God and God knows everything, I believe He was offering us a tantalizing sign. He ordained that this date would not be set in stone because, in His Sovereign Mercy, He is not willing that any should perish. Perhaps by His tarrying ("by the space of 40 metaphorical years?") all would have adequate time to repent during this "forty year wilderness walk."

> *The Lord is not slow to fulfill His promise as some understand slowness, but is patient with you, not wanting anyone to perish but everyone to come to repentance.*
> ~ 2 Peter 3:9 (Berean Study Bible)

For those of us who already love Christ, we are not to "worry" about this. As we wait, we labor as the Bride of Christ like the Proverbs 31 wife:

> *Give her of the fruit of her hands; and let her own works praise her in the gates.* ~ Proverbs 31:31 (NKJV)

Let's repent of any practices that have mimicked and mocked true works of the hand and instead are simply more examples of worthless...

Hand wringing.

Repentance Prayer:

Heavenly Father, Please forgive me for the times I knowingly or unknowingly adopted secular counterfeit spiritual practices in the hopes of gaining a fabricated sense of spiritual power. I REPENT for the ways in which I have attempted to manipulate objects as a channel for delving into the spiritual realm. Moving onward help me to see the sneaky schemes of the devil. Prepare me for battle relying solely on Your Power, equipped with the armor of God and following Your battle plan. Fill my mind with humility to obey You and submit to Your authority in all things. Teach me to pray, not by rote or ritualistically, but in the manner prescribed by our Lord and Savior, Jesus Christ. ~ Amen

Scriptures to help me cleanse with His Word:

_____

_____

_____

Pastor Jeffrey Daly

DAY #29
Step It Up
Give An Arm and a Leg?

40 Years King David Reigned Over Israel

Therefore, since we are surrounded by such a great cloud of witnesses, let us throw off every encumbrance and the sin that so easily entangles, and let us run with endurance the race set out for us. ~ Hebrews 12:1 (Berean Study Bible)

In our continuing devotional series of the "40/40's" in scripture, we come upon the Royal reign of David which lasted for forty years. David's reign began when God "rent" the Throne from Saul.

Once again this is a bible story that is too long to cover in detail today, but suffice it to say that Saul did not complete the task that God asked of him.

> *Now go and smite Amalek, and utterly destroy all that they have, and spare them not* ~ 1 Samuel 15:3(a) (KJV)

> *But Saul...spared Agag* ~ 1 Samuel 15: 9(a) (KJV)

The prophet Samuel was so upset by Saul's disobedience that he cried to the Lord all night! (1 Samuel 15:11 NKJV). Samuel then rebuked Saul on his failure to obey God:

> *Now the Lord sent you on a mission, and said, "Go, and utterly destroy the sinners, the Amalekites, and fight against them*

until they are consumed. Why then did you not obey the voice of the Lord? ~ 1 Samuel 15:18-19 (NKJV, emphasis added)

Samuel concluded:

> *To obey is better than sacrifice...rebellion is as the sin of WITCHCRAFT, and stubbornness is as iniquity and idolatry...Because you have rejected the Word of the Lord, He also has rejected you from being king...The Lord has given it to a neighbor of yours, who is better than you...*
> (excerpts from 1 Samuel 15: 22,23 & 28 (NKJV, emphasis added)

Saul admitted he had feared the people and had obeyed their voice and so the kingdom was given to David who, of course, is a foreshadowing of Christ Himself.

Today in our continuing theme of the Body of Christ "body parts"...let's talk about our arms and legs. I love the scripture verse up above in the heading. In other versions "the sin that so easily entangles us," is also translated as "the sin that so easily trips us up." (NIV). The scripture is so vivid. I envision arms and legs flailing about as we tumble head over heels.

At first glance, this judgment seems rather harsh on Saul. I mean didn't he "almost, sort of" do the job? In God's Olympian battle, Saul was attempting to play the spiritual "hokey-pokey." He thought he could just put his right arm in, his right arm out, his right leg in and shake it all about.

God has set a task before us and we must complete it! We must overcome if we want the prize.

> *Do you not know that in a race all the runners run, but only one receives the prize? Run in such a way as to take the prize.*
> ~ 1 Corinthians 9:24 (Berean Study Bible)

Pastor Jeffrey Daly

Revelation doesn't speak of "also rans" but of overcomers.

> *To him who overcomes I will grant to sit with Me on My Throne, as I also overcame and sat down with My Father on His Throne.* ~ Revelation 3:21 (NKJV)

Some people say that Saul's sin to finish the job with the Amalekites (who represent all sinners) had huge ramifications for the Israelites up the road. By sparing King Agag of the Amalekites, he allowed a line of people to continue which resulted in Haman who is listed in Esther 3:1 as the son of Hammedatha the Agagite! Haman is a shadow type of Satan and, in the story of Esther, he attempted to completely eradicate the Jews. We need to trust that God knows best...Haman (aka Satan), unlike Saul, went out to finish the job!

It was because of Esther's full obedience to God that the devil's mission ultimately failed. One person being obedient...that's what God requires and demands.

We must understand that our disobedience is likened unto witchcraft in scripture. It's "man's arm power" instead of relying on the unfailing arm of God.

There are no "also rans" at the Marriage Supper of the Lamb. If we want to dance with Christ at the greatest wedding party of all time, no hokey-pokey allowed.

He wants a partner who is "all in."

Repentance Prayer:

Heavenly Father, Please forgive me for the times I disobeyed You and listened to other voices. Please forgive me for the times I feared man instead of You. I REPENT for the ways in which I have attempted to wield spiritual power in my own strength instead of relying upon Your Power. Moving onward teach me to obey right away, all the way so that I might finish the task You have set before me. Prepare me for battle using Your directions, equipped with the armor of God and following Your battle plan. Fill my mind with humility to obey You and submit to Your authority in all things. Help me to be completely committed to You and You alone. I pray this prayer in the Name above all names, the King of kings, the Lord of lords, YESHUA. ~ Amen

Scriptures to help me cleanse with His Word:

_____

_____

_____

DAY #30
Get Under Your Skin
Body Odor

40 Years King Solomon Reigned Over Israel

God is Spirit, and His worshipers must worship Him in spirit and in truth.   ~ John 4:24 (Berean Study Bible)

In our continuing devotional series of the "40/40's" in scripture, we come upon the Reign of Solomon. For forty years, Solomon reigned over a yet undivided Israel.

When most people think of Solomon, we automatically think of him as a "good" and "wise" king of Israel. He was, of course, another shadow-picture of Christ who was to come. However, as all fleshly Bible characters, he left a lot to be desired.

I'm not sure that there is a sadder chapter in all of scripture history than 1 Kings 11. Perhaps you have never even noticed it. I urge you to read the entire chapter, but allow me to put some of the "low"-lights excerpted below:

> *But King Solomon loved many foreign women*
> *Solomon clung to these in love.*
> *For it came to pass, when Solomon was old, that his wives turned away his heart after other gods.*
> *For Solomon went after Ashtoreth...after Milcom...*

> Then did Solomon build a high place for Chemosh...and
> for Molech.
> And likewise did he for all his strange wives, which burnt
> incense and sacrificed unto their gods.
>
> Kings 11:1-8 (NKJV)

Wow...think about this. Solomon actually built monuments and sacrificed to demon gods. I bet we would all fail to get this correct on a Bible proficiency exam!

To give you an idea of how evil this was in the sight of God, here's some quick info on what these wicked demon-gods represent:

<u>Ashtoreth</u>: *Female goddess worship, over-exaltation of women power.*

<u>Milcom</u>: *National god. Worship of political power.*

<u>Chemosh</u>: *The god of SELF focus. False confidence, audacity, worship of the temple itself.*

<u>Molech:</u> *Required the sacrifice of your very own children.*

It was because of Solomon's disobedience that the entire nation of Israel was rent in two after his death.

Once again I am brought to my knees with the painful awareness of how easy it seems to get tripped up in sin. If the wisest human in all of history can't get it straight, what hope is there for you and me? Do we, or our nations, make "altars and sacrifices" to women's reproductive powers, political power, church power and, ultimately, sacrifice the future of our very own children? Wait a minute. Hmmmm....

> *O wretched man I am! Who will deliver me out of this body of*
> *death? Thanks be to God, through Jesus Christ our Lord!*
> ~ Romans 7:24-25 (Berean Literal Bible)

In many spiritual rituals, incense is often used. However, does God *really* want these types of outward shows of offerings?

> ...*Does the Lord delight in burnt offerings and sacrifices as much as in obeying the voice of the LORD? Behold, obedience is better than sacrifice, and attentiveness is better than the fat of rams.* ~ 1 Samuel 15:22 (Berean Study Bible)

During the Feast of Tabernacles (Sukkot), the children of Israel were instructed to make "lulavs." Lulavs are bundled branches of palm fronds, myrtle, and willow along with an "etrog." The etrog (or lemon) is said to look like the human heart. The Israelites would wave these bundles to signify a pleasing sacrifice, or smell, unto the Lord.

Interestingly, lime (not lemon) is used to cover over the smell of death. Even to this very day it is used in forensics and homicide scenes. The word "limelight" describes someone in the public eye receiving praise and attention. When we are intent on living in the "limelight" we are not walking in Life with Christ, but simply covering over the smell of death. We need to worship God on the inside, in our spirit, and not just have an outward show, lest we be likened by Christ unto whitened tombs full of the stench of rotting flesh.

> ...*For you are like tombs having been whitewashed, which indeed outwardly appear beautiful, but inside they are full of bones of the dead, and of all impurity.* ~ Matthew 23:27 (Berean Literal Bible)

Instead, God wants to smell the "lemon" of our pure hearts. The pleasing aroma created with the Etrog (lemon), palm fronds (easily moved by the Wind of the Holy Spirit), myrtle (faithfulness) and willow (sorrow for our sins), are all joined together as a pleasing incense to the Lord.

During our repentance time, let's make sure we don't fail...

The Heavenly sniff test.

Repentance Prayer:

Heavenly Father, We acknowledge that we have amassed wealth, power and spiritual pride instead of humility. Please write your Law upon our hearts and help us to learn it every day so that we might not sin against You. The lust of the eye, the lust of the flesh and the pride of life continue to tempt us. Please call us to be watchful and renounce these temptations and to turn away today to pursue Your Holiness. Help us to be a sweet smell unto You instead of a stink (Isaiah 3:24 KJV). As the Body of Christ, help us to remove Body Odor through obedience and transform us with Your purity. And finally, help us to walk in Love, as Christ also has loved us and gave Himself for us as an offering and a sacrifice to God for a sweet-smelling aroma. (Ephesians 5:2 NKJV). We pray this prayer in the Name above all names, the King of all kings, the Lord of lords, Yeshua, our Lord and Savior. ~ Amen

Scriptures to help me cleanse with His Word:

_____

_____

_____

DAY #31
Intestinal Fortitude
Gut Wrenching

40 Sockets of Silver to Build the Temple

Do you not know that your body is a temple of the Holy Spirit who is in you, whom you have received from God? You are not your own, ~ 1 Corinthians 6:19 (Berean Study Bible)

Did you ever take the time to closely read in Exodus the meticulously detailed blueprints for building the Temple? If you haven't, I encourage you to do so. The Temple is a metaphor for the Body of Christ in which the Holy Spirit of God dwells...fearfully and wonderfully made.

I will praise Thee; for I am fearfully and wonderfully made: marvelous are Thy works. ~ Psalm 139:14 (KJV)

In our continuing devotional series on the "40/40's" found in scripture, today we marvel at the forty Sockets of Silver that were required in the Temple (Exodus 36:25-25 KJV). The temple sockets were made to hold the corresponding gold-pronged temple walls which fit neatly into the sockets. The silver sockets represent a "hidden foundation"...the veiled Bride of Christ.

Our bodies are, indeed, our temples. When we meditate on God "in the temple" we literally have *temples* on our heads between which lies our physical brain meditating! God is hilarious.

In our "Body of Christ Presentation Chart," let's consider the "guts" or "bowels."

> For the king of Babylon stands at the fork in the road, at the junction of the two roads, to seek an omen: He shakes the arrows, he consults the idols, he examines the liver.
> ~ Ezekiel 21:21 (Berean Study Bible, emphasis added)

Interestingly, the "liver" in scripture has more of the meaning of what we today would call the "heart." As we see in Ezekiel 21:21 LIVERS were actually used in the occult practice of divination. It is located centrally in men's "inner guts." In scripture, God has a lot to say about examining inner guts but not through the spiritual counterfeit of divination.

We see Judas' guts discussed here:

With the reward of his wickedness Judas bought a field, and falling headlong, he burst open in the middle and all his intestines spilled out. ~ Acts 1:18 (Berean Study Bible, emphasis added)

And here again in the Old Testament with King Belshazzar, Nebuchadnezzar's son:

> Then the king's countenance was changed, and his thoughts troubled him, so that the joints of his loins were loosed, and his knees smote one against another.
> ~ Daniel 5:6 (KJV, emphasis added)

These scripture show God revealing what was in the "inner man." Peter was not encouraging Christ when he said:

> "Far be it from You, Lord!" "This shall never happen to You!"
> ~ Matthew 16:22(b) (Berean Study Bible)

According to popular Christian lingo, wasn't Peter merely "speaking life?" Yet, Jesus called him SATAN. Wow. Jesus goes right to the gut of the matter.

Surely by now Peter knew better than to go against what Yeshua, the Messiah, the Son of the Living God, told him. In a selfish desire for personal comfort, Peter had the audacity to "divine" something other than God's Sovereign Plan. This occurs just a few short verses after making his God-inspired divine confession of belief!

The difference here is this: Is the "divination" or prediction designed to tickle ears or divinely inspired to strengthen up the Body of Christ? Does it "shore up" the Body of Christ or tear it down? Peter's words, if hearkened to, were flesh-divined to deflate Christ's *resolve* (aka guts).

Today, many in the church are pointing out portentous signs: earthly wars, spiritual battles, earthquakes, and famines.

Does this make our bowels quake?

For those with unrepentant sin in their lives, prophecy fulfillment may create a queasy gut feeling. Thank God, there is still time to REPENT. For the repentant, it is simply one more indication that our Lord and Savior is soon to return. Like Paul, we feel a yearning:

> *For God is my record, how greatly I long after you all in the bowels of Jesus Christ.* ~ Philippians 1:8 (KJV)

So, don't look down. It will upset your stomach. Look up...

for your redemption draweth nigh.

Repentance Prayer:

Heavenly Father, Please forgive us for failing to see you as the only firm Foundation. Help us to only speak words that strengthen the resolve of your Church and provide much needed support. Let us not construct anything that is not tried and tested to pass Your inspection. Forgive us for the times when we participated in any flimsy spiritual counterfeits. Fortify our inner man as Your temple and keep us protected from the evil one. We pray this in the Name above all names, the King of kings, the Lord of lords, Jesus Christ our Lord and Savior. ~ Amen

Scriptures to help me cleanse with His Word:

_____

_____

_____

DAY #32
Time's Up
Raise The Alarm

40 Days Nineveh had to Repent or be Overthrown

What meanest thou, O sleeper. Arise, call upon thy God.
~ Jonah 1:6 (KJV)

In today's "40/40" we all remember the Bible story of Jonah. Jonah was a prophet called by God to tell Nineveh that they had forty days to repent or they would be overturned.

"Yet forty days and Nineveh shall be overthrown."
~ Jonah 3:4 (KJV)

When we look at the sins of our nations today, I think many lack a sense of urgency. Far too many people think we can continue indefinitely down the pathway of serious sin. Maybe we are thinking: *"Sure...it would be nice to overthrow abortion sometime in our lifetime"...YAWWWWN." Hopefully it will get done. Goin' back to sleep now."*

This position is both dangerous and arrogant. Nazi Germany was reduced to rubble and destroyed in just twelve years after they began innocent slaughter at the Death Camps between 1933-1945. Surely we are on borrowed time.

In the scripture, we see a sense of urgency in Justice.

And they cried out in a loud voice, "How long, O Lord, holy and true, until You judge those who live on the earth and avenge our blood?" ~ Revelation 6:10 (Berean Study Bible)

Innocent blood cries out to the Lord for response:

"What have you done?" replied the LORD. "The voice of your brother's blood cries out to Me from the ground.
~ Genesis 4:10 (Berean Study Bible)

To complete our focus on the "Body of Christ presentation chart," today we will discuss the feet. We will round out this study in the next four devotionals with "Body functions" to wrap up the entire analogy for the Body of Christ.

What do "feet" represent in the scripture? Jesus washed the disciples' feet in preparation for the Great Commission.

As it is written: "How beautiful are the feet of those who bring good news! ~ Romans 10:15(b) (NIV)

The word "gospel" literally means "Good News!" Remember, the good news, as taught by both John the Baptist and Jesus Christ, was preceded by one single word: REPENT.

The spiritual counterfeit for gospel feet would be summed up by "dreamers." The word "dreamers" only shows up twice in the New King James scripture, once in the Old Testament and once in the New Testament. In both verses the word is used in a negative sense.

When Jeremiah vented against all the false practitioners who were unwisely advising the king, "dreamers" made the Top 5 hit-list:

Therefore hearken not ye to your prophets, nor to your diviners, <u>nor to your dreamers,</u> nor to your enchanters, nor to your sorcerers ~Jeremiah 27:9(a) (KJV, emphasis added)

Jude, the brother of Christ, goes even further and calls them filthy dreamers:

> Likewise also these <u>filthy dreamers</u> defile the flesh, despise dominion, and speak evil of dignities.
> ~ Jude 1:8 (KJV, emphasis added)

Wow!...Who and *What* does this describe so we can avoid this ungodly practice? Since Joseph had dreams which were clearly God-ordained, obviously this is not the same thing. These are *self*-created dreams or *self*-delusions.

In both scriptural instances, these verses refer to continuing blindly on the pathway of sin and self-deception. I urge you to read both chapters fully.

Sin is toxic. Sin is the equivalent of cancer in the Body of Christ. The same applies to our nations. Like cancer, it metastasizes. As it progresses, the Body is ravaged and wasted. If we were giving a medical prognosis: We only have a certain amount of time left to live. Sin cancer will lay us flat out.

So, when we hear the national call for repentance, do we arise and answer this call or keep dreaming? One thing is certain...the snooze button for "dreamers" is not an indefinite option. Like Nineveh, the clock is ticking. We either get down on our knees or we will get our feet knocked out from under us.

The scripture is clear: Humble ourselves or be humbled by God Almighty. Either way, we're going down...

Let's hit the ground repenting.

Repentance Prayer:

Heavenly Father, I REPENT for my apathy and lack of urgency in rescuing those being led away to death, and for not holding back those staggering towards slaughter. Fill us with courage to speak out and resist evil. Forgive us for the times when we participated in any flimsy spiritual counterfeits that encouraged people to go back to sleep instead of waking up. Help us to get on our feet to lead others off the pathway of destruction and then get down on our knees to REPENT. We pray this in the Name above all names, the King of kings, the Lord of lords, Jesus Christ our Lord and Savior. ~ Amen

Scriptures to help me cleanse with His Word:

_____

_____

_____

Pastor Jeffrey Daly

DAY #33
Eating Humble Pie
An Acquired Taste

40 Days Ezekiel Laid on His Right
Side to Symbolize Judah's Sins

So I went to the angel, telling him to give me the little book. And he said to me, "Take it and eat it; it will make your stomach bitter, but in your mouth it will be sweet as honey." I took the little book out of the angel's hand and ate it, and in my mouth it was sweet as honey; and when I had eaten it, my stomach was made bitter. ~ Revelation 10:9-10 (NASB)

Just when I think I've studied the strangest story in scripture, another one freshly amazes me. In Ezekiel 4 we see the prophet Ezekiel, at the Lord's instruction, building a little diorama scene of Jerusalem. From the wording, it sounds exactly like today's equivalent of toy soldiers, complete with battering rams, siege walls and ramparts. This story, in another translation (MSG), is entitled:

"This Is What Sin Does."

During the entire 430 days (390 for Israel and 40 for Judah...which corresponds with our study of the 40/40's in scripture), Ezekiel had to lay on his side bound with ropes, eating food cooked on dung, in order to physically act out this diorama spectacle. Can God make His illustrations any more dramatic in order to get their attention?

And when thou hast accomplished them, lie again on thy right side, and thou shalt bear the iniquity of the house of Judah forty days. ~ Ezekiel 4:6(a) (KJV, emphasis added)

Fast forward to modern day: What does it take for us to see what God is obviously spelling out for us? We are under spiritual siege, bound up and eating filth!

Does it take Drag Queen story hour?

How about Satan Baphomet Coloring Books in the Public Schools?

An Atheist Monument at Courthouse next to The Ten commandments?

Graphic sex acts taught to your children in "sex ed" class?

Baby body parts for sale on-line?

Christians going to jail for teaching the Bible?

Christian Adoption agencies forced to close or give children to gays?

Children getting sex changes without your permission?

Sex change clinics now opening for children as young as FIVE?

Children being euthanized?

Sadly, this list could continue as there is a new shocker every day. Have we simply gone numb like those in Ezekiel's day? How long will we be able to digest this garbage?

In today's continued theme on the Body of Christ, we discuss the digestive system. As Ezekiel so blatantly portrayed, how much junk do we have to consume before we realize we are becoming very ill as a society? When does this make us sick to our stomachs?

The scripture gives us the antidote.

Instead of simply taking in all of this "food cooked on dung" why don't we publicly and nationally eat some humble pie?

That's why it's time for a public declaration of National Repentance in every nation where there are believers in Christ; those who are His people, called by His Name. Let's be like Ezekiel. Let's publicly and dramatically REPENT to reveal that the Church is currently bound up, knocked on its side and ingesting uncleanness.

If not, this "Toy Story" is going to get all too real.

Repentance Prayer:

Heavenly Father, I REPENT for becoming accustomed and conformed to the evil around me instead of fulfilling Your Great Commission, Fill us with courage to speak out and resist evil. Forgive us for the times when we participated in any flimsy spiritual counterfeits that encouraged people to remain bound up, ineffective and ingesting uncleanness. Help us to be loosed from bondage, standing upright and eating The Bread of Life. Help us to REPENT and then lead others off the pathway of destruction. We pray this in the Name above all names, the King of kings, the Lord of lords, Jesus Christ our Lord and Savior. ~ Amen

Scriptures to help me cleanse with His Word:

_____

_____

_____

Pastor Jeffrey Daly

DAY #34
Resistance Training
Mud Wrestling

40 Days Jesus Fasted in the Wilderness

Every athlete exercises self-control in all things. They do it to receive a perishable wreath, but we an imperishable.
~ 1 Corinthians 9:25 (ESV)

Today we come upon another "40/40" in scripture:

Then Jesus was led up by the Spirit into the wilderness to be tempted by the devil. And when He had fasted forty days and forty nights, afterward He was hungry.
~ Matthew 4:1-2 (NKJV)

There's a common myth among the fitness crowd that fasting causes a wasting away of your muscle mass. This has been shown to be utterly untrue. Muscle mass is a function of exercise. Nutritionists will tell us that we cannot "eat our way" to more muscles. Anyone who has attempted to do this has become clearly aware of this Truth! Their "muscle mass" looks suspiciously like a flabby gut.

Once again, in our "Body Functions" of the Body of Christ, this is an apt analogy for another spiritual counterfeit. Somehow in the "faith alone" doctrine we've gotten lazy. If we don't "work it out" we are not going to grow strong muscles in Christ.

The spiritual counterfeit illustrated today is "calling on the dead." Mediums are an abomination in scripture as Solomon said below:

> *Whatever your hand finds to <u>do, do it with all your might,</u> for in the realm of the dead, where you are going, there is neither working nor planning nor knowledge nor wisdom.*
> ~ Ecclesiastes 9:10 (NIV, emphasis added)

Since the cross-bearing persecutions of the First Century Church, it seems that man has attempted to find an easier way to enter the Kingdom. Whether through a series of rote, minimal-effort steps, distorted philosophies or misguided positive thinking, the results have been disastrous. If the pulpit coaches were getting a grade from the Lord God Almighty on winning the world for Christ, an "F" for "flabby" might be appropriate here. Clearly the church has conformed more to the world than vice versa. We need to get off the pew and get exercised about the dying and lost world around us.

You and I are tempted to want the path of least resistance. We often want an "extreme makeover" with little to no effort...the equivalent of a spiritual plastic surgery. Perhaps we think we can become spiritual powerhouses simply by weekly church injections. We must be tried and tested now. With Jesus as our Perfect Role Model, our "mettle" must be tested on earth if we want to get the "medal" later.

I'm no fan of mud wrestling, but for today it works as a great analogy. We need to wrestle with our mud, not simply stay in it. When the prodigal son finally got out of the pigsty, he had to pull himself out of the sticky slop with both mental and physical effort, the very definition of REPENT. Mentally change your mind (Greek: metanoia) and physically turn around (Hebrew: shuv).

Very few people read this scripture in Luke 15 (KJV, emphasis added) carefully. Here are the clarifying excerpts:

> *Verse 17: And when he came to himself*
> *[Mental effort]*

Verse 18: I will arise and go to my father
[Mental effort acknowledging that physical action is required]

Verse 20: And he arose, and came to his father. [Action]

We already have the "club membership" but in order for it to make a difference, we must get going! Note that, the father, a shadow picture of our Father in Heaven, did not meet up with him *until* he was on the *road*. This is a very important distinction. Even more amazing is this next verse. It states that the prodigal was <u>dead</u> to the father:

> *For this my son was dead, and is alive again; he was lost, and*
> *is found.* ~ Luke 15:24(a) (KJV, emphasis added)

Jesus wrestled the devil during His road trip through the wilderness. Jesus' previous forty days in the spiritual exercise of fasting did not waste Him away, but strengthened Him. He had "resistance training."

> *Resist the devil and he will flee from you.*
> ~ James 4:7(b) (NKJV)

The testing has begun. Soon there will be the final "try-outs." Then comes the Olympian Battle. Those who think they can just sit it out in the pews and still be in shape will simply...

Get dragged through the mud.

> *Because we have these promises, dear friends, let us cleanse*
> *ourselves from everything that can defile our body or spirit.*
> *And let us work toward complete purity because we fear God.*
> ~2 Corinthians 7:1 (NLT)

Repentance Prayer:

Heavenly Father, I REPENT for wallowing around in the mud instead of walking towards You. Let me not be considered "dead to the Father" and of no use in your Kingdom battle. Help me to GO and make disciples of all nations. Fill me with strong spiritual muscles as I submit to your resistance training. Forgive me for the times when I was spiritually lazy. Help us to REPENT and then lead others off the pathway of destruction. We pray this in the Name above all names, the King of kings, the Lord of lords, Jesus Christ our Lord and Savior. ~ Amen

Scriptures to help me cleanse with His Word:

_____

_____

_____

Pastor Jeffrey Daly

DAY #35
Get the Blood Pumping
Appear In Circulation

40 Days Jesus Appeared to His
Followers after His Resurrection

*On that day a fountain will be opened to the house of David
and the residents of Jerusalem, to cleanse them from sin and
impurity.* ~ Zechariah 13:1 (Berean Study Bible)

In our continuing devotional study of the "40/40's" found in scripture, we come to Acts 1:3. Scripture tells us that Jesus appeared publicly to His followers for forty days after His resurrection and before His ascension.

Today, we also discuss the spiritual counterfeit of astrology. There is probably no more obvious testament to God's Glory in creation than the Heavens.

*The Heavens declare the Glory of God; the skies proclaim the
work of His Hands.* ~ Psalm 19:1 (NIV)

The precision-like rotations of the planets in orbit and the order of the vast galaxies are beyond our comprehension. It is understandable that one would want to consult the Heavens for spiritual inspiration.

Astrology seeks occult knowledge from the "circulatory system" in the skies. The term "circulatory system" also refers to the pumping of Blood throughout the Body, a great metaphor for our Body Functions analogy.

Why did Jesus remain for forty days on planet Earth before His ascension into the Heavens? If I may be so bold as to offer a theological opinion, it was because He knew that the scattered disciples needed to be brought back into spiritual alignment.

In the wondrous synchronicity of the Holy Scripture, we see twelve post-resurrection appearances to His followers mentioned just as there were twelve original disciples. In this very same chapter of Acts 1, which mentions the forty days of Jesus' earthly post-resurrection appearances, we see that something is "out of alignment."

There are only *eleven* disciples remaining since Judas' innards spilled in the Field of Blood. In Acts 1, a new disciple is chosen to replace the vacancy left by Judas, the betrayer.

In an amazing representation of God's Grace through Jesus Christ, the two men chosen for consideration were named "Justus" and "Matthias." By God's orderly alignment (and not spiritual counterfeits like astrology or Hindu chakras), Matthias was chosen by lot. Without getting too lengthy for our short devotionals, "lots" represent choosing parcels for tillage. God is constantly seeking "suitable" soil to extend His Kingdom. "Adam" literally means "red dirt" or "blood man."

In a mind-blowing move which can only come about from God's Sovereign Majesty, the names "Justus" and "Matthias" are translated as "Justice" and "Mercy." We know that "Matthias" (Mercy) was Divinely chosen to represent Christ's shed Blood on the Cross. When organizing His disciples back into "alignment," this amazing Bible story shows us that instead of getting what we deserve (lawful judgment), we instead receive a gift of God's Mercy through the Blood of Jesus Christ.

So don't study the skies for a spiritual counterfeit, but instead keep watching for our Blessed Hope in Christ's Second Coming.

> *"Men of Galilee," they said, "Why do you stand here looking into the sky? This same Jesus, who has been taken from you*

into heaven, will come back in the same way you have seen Him
go into heaven." ~ Acts 1:11 (NIV)

In leaving us with Mercy instead of Justice, we no longer have to be under the curse of a "horror"-scope. In His Goodness, he has substituted the lasting shame of the "Field of Blood" legacy of Judas for His Mercy. Yeshua's forty days on Earth "got the Blood pumping" from the Cross. It is the Mercy fountain that continues to this day.

Will you immerse yourself in His circulating Blood now? If we reject His Gift of Mercy, instead our "lot," like Judas, will be Divine Judgment.

And whosoever was not found written in the Book of Life was
cast in the Lake of Fire. ~ Revelation 20:15 (KJV)

I don't know about you but I desire Mercy! Let's REPENT!

But go and learn what this means: "I desire mercy, not
sacrifice." For I have not come to call the righteous, but sinners
to repentance." ~Matthew 9:13 (NKJV)

Repentance Prayer:

Heavenly Father, I REPENT for being out of Your Holy alignment. Forgive me for looking to spiritual counterfeits instead of keeping my eyes focused on You. Help me to accept the wondrous Gift of Your Mercy offered at the Cross beginning with REPENTANCE. I turn away from my thoughts and my ways to The Only Way of the Blood of Jesus Christ. Let me not attempt to use false spiritual power that is of no use in Your Kingdom battle. Help me to GO and make disciples of all nations. Help us to REPENT and then lead others off the pathway of destruction. We pray this in the Name above all names, the King of kings, the Lord of lords, Jesus Christ our Lord and Savior. ~ Amen

Scriptures to help me cleanse with His Word:

_____

_____

_____

Pastor Jeffrey Daly

DAY #36
Ashes, Ashes, We All Fall Down
Beauty and the Beast

40 Symbolic Years in a Biblical Generation

Your eyes will see the King in His beauty; They will behold a
far-distant land. ~ Isaiah 33:17 (NASB)

For our next devotional, in our continuing series of the "40/40's" found within scripture, we come to the generally accepted principle that there are forty years in a biblical generation. Now, as far as I can tell, there is not one single scripture that states definitively how many years a "generation" is and theological estimates range from a low of twenty (Numbers 14:29 NKJV) to a high of 120 years (Genesis 6:3 NKJV). Then, where does this concept of forty years come from?

In Matthew 24:34 (ESV), when Christ stated "this generation will not pass away," we know from Josephus' first-hand account of history, that forty years later the Temple in Jerusalem was destroyed. Of course, Matthew 24 is speaking both contemporaneously and prophetically as well. The word "generation" is "genea" in the Greek. While it means "a multitude of men living at the same time" it also means "that which has been begotten, men of the same stock, a family." Thus, Christ's "family" or "genealogy" does not pass away until all of Matthew 24 has been utterly fulfilled on Earth. The forty years of a biblical generation symbolizes mankind's wilderness trek on planet Earth until the return of His Second Coming.

In today's "spiritual counterfeit" study, we discuss those who practice "secret arts." When we think of secret arts, it brings to mind smoke and mirrors...false illusions...cheap imitation appearing real.

> *So Moses and Aaron went to Pharaoh and did just as the LORD commanded. Aaron cast down his staff before Pharaoh and his servants, and it became a serpent. Then Pharaoh summoned the wise men and the sorcerers, and they, the magicians of Egypt, <u>also did the same by their secret arts.</u> For each man cast down his staff, and they became serpents. But Aaron's staff swallowed up their staffs.*
> ~Exodus 7:10-12 (ESV, emphasis added).

In the ongoing analogy of the Body Functions of the Body of Christ, our final focus today is on the Respiratory System. While I am not advocating Gothic rock music, there is a popular song entitled: *"Bring Me To Life"* by Evanescence. As everything in the world ultimately brings Glory to God, whether intended or not, the lyrics speak of our core deadness until Love brings us to Life (in an album appropriately entitled "Fallen").

God's Love brings us to Life. In Genesis, we see a shadow picture of this spiritual rebirth as God brings Adam to life:

> *Then the LORD God formed man from the dust of the ground and breathed the breath of life into his nostrils, and the man became a living being.* ~ Genesis 2:7 (Berean Study Bible)

Throughout great literature, we see this repeat story-line of the "fake" or "dead" (non-breathing, non-spirit filled) become "real" or "alive" (breathing, spirit-filled). The Velveteen Rabbit became real through the love of a child. Pinocchio became real through the love of the Father. In Pygmalion, we see a statue become real through the love of the Artist who then marries her! This is great symbolism for Christ and His Bride.

Those of us who are in the family ("genea") of Yeshua, have His Spirit breathed into us. God is not a practitioner of "secret arts." This family relationship should be clearly evident to all those around us. Those with God's Holy Spirit breathed into them should be as obvious as the difference between those who are breathing and those who are not, as evident as Life and Death.

Ashes to ashes, dust to dust...

> *For dust you are, and to dust you shall return.*
> ~ Genesis 3:19(b) (NKJV)

Repentance is symbolized by ashes. Once we realize that we are sinners, we are reduced to ashes (repentance). However, we don't simply rise from our repentance ashes like a Phoenix, which is the pagan Egyptian concept much like Pharaoh's cheap imitation staffs. What is the "beauty" we receive?

> *One thing I have asked from the LORD, that I shall seek: That I may dwell in the House of the LORD all the days of my life, to behold the beauty of the LORD and to meditate in His Temple.*
> ~ Psalm 27:4 (NASB, emphasis added)

He is the Beauty. Without Him, We are the Beast.

> *I said to myself, "As for the sons of men, God tests them so that they may see for themselves that they are but beasts."*
> ~ Ecclesiastes 3:18 (Berean Study Bible)

When we, through repentance, admit the deadness of our human beastliness, He uses our ashes to create a...

Master Peace.

Repentance Prayer:

Heavenly Father, I REPENT for thinking I am the Beauty instead of gazing at Your Beauty, Lord. Forgive me for looking to spiritual counterfeits instead of keeping my eyes focused on You. It is through Your Holy Spirit that we have our breath and come to life. Help me to accept the wondrous Gift of Your Transformation beginning with REPENTANCE. I turn away from my thoughts and my ways to The Only Way of the Blood of Jesus Christ through the Power of the Holy Spirit. Help me to GO and make disciples of all nations. Help us to REPENT and then lead others off the pathway of destruction. We pray this in the Name above all names, the King of kings, the Lord of lords, Jesus Christ our Lord and Savior. ~ Amen

Scriptures to help me cleanse with His Word:

_____

_____

_____

DAY #37
At Death's Door
Under No Delusions

40 Years after Crucifixion, Destruction of the Temple

Then Jesus went out and departed from the temple, and His disciples came up to show Him the buildings of the temple. And Jesus said to them, "Do you not see all these things? Assuredly, I say to you, not one stone shall be left here upon another, that shall not be thrown down." ~ Matthew 24:1-2 (NKJV)

It could not be more appropriate today that we reach the topic of "Destruction of the Temple." It is an apt metaphor for innocent slaughter. When we destroy another human being, we are destroying a temple.

At this point in our devotionals, we might be tempted to say "what a long strange trip it's been." With thirty-six devotionals behind us we have covered:

7 Things the Lord Hates
7 Deadly Sins
10 Commandments
12 Spiritual Counterfeits in the Body of Christ

Our final four Devotionals will focus on The Four National Apostasies that destroyed ancient Israel as a nation. These four national sins have the potential to lead our modern day nations into the same path of bondage and destruction. They are:

1) **Innocent Slaughter** ~(aka destruction of God's Temple)
2) Sanctification of Perversions
3) Removal and then Replacement of God Almighty in the public square and in the churches
4) Betrayal of the Throne of David

We can almost palpably feel the spiritual intensity building, the bells ringing, the shofars sounding, as we discuss these Final Four National Sins.

As a global population, we move "Forward" to born-alive abortions, euthanasia of children, the disabled, the terminally ill and the elderly. Is there anyone not on the hit-list "marked for death?" Apparently not. As cleric and poet John Donne so succinctly stated: *"Ask not for whom the bell tolls, it tolls for thee."* How much longer before you and your loved ones fall into the class of those deemed undesirable?

In embracing our "Hebrew Roots" we are simply acknowledging His Truth made evident in the Old Testament practices. It is not our intent to return to legalism or any "first covenant" practices which do not mention Yeshua or His prophetic fulfillment. We instead want to show how every Word from Genesis through Revelation is about Him and His sacrificial love for us.

For instance, when we observe Passover, we don't simply observe a ritualistic Passover, but Jesus Christ in the symbolism of the Passover. This is an incredibly important distinction as we see a new obsession with the Third Temple rebuild and its attendant animal sacrifices.

People may innocently ask: *"What's the difference? Isn't that simply embracing another shadow-picture of what is to come in Christ's Second Coming?"*

Thus, many Christians may herald a Third Temple rebuild as an exciting development indicating that the return of Jesus Christ is closer than ever.

However, so too would the appearance of the "man of lawlessness" and a spirit of anti-Christ! While some things are prophesied to happen, we must be careful of what we support.

Any "Hebrew Roots" celebrations must be centered around the proclamation of Yeshua. The Old Testament was a "shadow-picture" of Christ and now we must proclaim Him to the world, not retreat back into the shadows.

He told us to practice communion "in remembrance" of Him. He did not tell us to continue slaughtering innocent animals "in remembrance" of Him!

> *For it is impossible for those who were once enlightened, and have tasted the Heavenly Gift, and have become partakers of the Holy Spirit, and have tasted the Good Word of God [Jesus is the Good Word] and the powers of the age to come, if they fall away, to renew them again to repentance, since they <u>crucify again</u> for themselves the Son of God, and put Him to an open shame.* ~ Hebrews 6:4-6 (NKJV, emphasis added)

> *By that will, we are having been sanctified through the offering of the body of Jesus Christ <u>once</u> for all.*
> ~Hebrews 10:10 (Berean Literal Bible, emphasis added)

> We are to preach CHRIST and CHRIST crucified.

In supporting Israel, our Godly root, we must explain to them that *they* become the Temple of God through Christ's sacrifice and the indwelling of His Holy Spirit.

> *...the Most High does not dwell in temples made with hands,*
> ~ Acts 7:48(a) (NKJV)

In the story of Rachel and Leah, Rachel trades intimacy with her husband Jacob for some of Leah's mandrakes. Certainly this is another one of the strangest stories in scripture!

A mandrake has two properties:

1) The only part that is not poisonous is the FRUIT
2) It contains hallucinogenic properties that cause DELIRIUM

The word *root* of "delirium" (pun intended) literally means to "deviate from the furrows." While He is definitely pouring out His Holy Spirit in these End Times, let's not become overly delirious with Hebrew Roots. We must not go off the straight furrow and narrow pathway of Salvation. Yeshua is the only Way, not another brick and stone Temple rebuild.

Let us not, with unforgivable forethought, be doing Satan's work and mark the Jewish people for destruction. If we enjoy uncovering prophetic knowledge through studying Hebrew Roots which point to Christ, we must, like Rachel, offer the Jewish people back their Bridegroom Yeshua for intimacy and Salvation.

Repentance Prayer:

Heavenly Father, I REPENT for any times I unknowingly participated in the potential spiritual slaughter of innocents. I turn away from my thoughts and my ways to the Only Way through the Blood of Jesus Christ. Let me not attempt to use false spiritual power that is of no use in Your Kingdom battle. Keep us from the powerful delusions of the evil one. Help me to GO and make disciples of all nations in the Name of Jesus Christ of Nazareth. Help us to REPENT and then lead others off the pathway of destruction. Enable us to teach that there is only One Name under Heaven and Earth by which men might be saved, His Name is Yeshua in whose Name we pray. ~ Amen

Scriptures to help me cleanse with His Word:

_____

_____

_____

DAY #38
So Over the Rainbow
Wave the Red Flag

40 Years of Age or Over was the Man
Healed by Peter and John

*Now therefore, please swear to me by the Lord that you will
indeed show kindness to my family because I showed kindness
to you. Give me a sure sign.*
~ Joshua 2:12 (Berean Study Bible)

Rahab the prostitute was most definitely "counter-cultural." In the documentary *Patterns of Evidence: The Exodus* (which I highly recommend watching, by the way), archaeological excavations of Jericho indicate that one small section of the wall did not completely collapse. Bible theorists hypothesize that this, perhaps, was the window of Rahab the prostitute. In the midst of utter societal collapse, one whore repenting and trusting in the God of Israel, saved herself and advanced the cause of the Israelites towards the Promised Land.

In today's continuing series of the "40/40's" found in scripture, we come to another unusual Bible Story.

> *When the rulers and Council members had threatened them*
> *further, they let them go, finding no way to punish them*
> *because [of their fear] of the people, for they were all praising*
> *and glorifying and honoring God for what had happened; for*

the man to whom this sign (attesting miracle) of healing had
happened <u>was more than forty years old</u>.
~ Acts 4:21-22 (AMP, emphasis added)

Huh? At first glance, this stumped me (which is probably not that hard to do!). Why was the Sanhedrin unable to punish Peter and John simply because the man was *"more than forty years old?"* What in the world does that have to do with anything?

The Sanhedrin Council meeting was convened because they wanted Peter and John to SHUT UP! In Acts Chapter 4, we see them boldly proclaiming the gospel of Jesus Christ and preaching the resurrection of the dead. This particular miracle (healing the man that was lame since birth) was causing such a widespread stir that the Council simply had to address it.

And a certain man <u>lame from his mother's womb</u> was carried,
whom they laid daily at the gate of the temple which is called
Beautiful.   ~ Acts 3:2 (NKJV, emphasis added)

In the 2nd of our Final 4 Devotionals on the 4 National Apostasies, we come to the "Sanctification of Perversions." What exactly is this national sin? In ancient times, it was made evident by bringing perverse sexual practices into the Temple. Remember Eli's sons from Devotional #23? I urge you to re-read that Devotional again today as it is incredibly pertinent to our discussion on National Apostasy #2. Eli's sons were having sex with prostitutes *in the Temple* (1 Samuel 2:22 NKJV). Temple prostitution may, indeed, be "the world's oldest profession," however God's punishment of this sin is very swift.

Fast forward to modern times. How do we commit this National Apostasy today? The United States Supreme Court case of *Obergefell* vs. *Hodges* is clearly an example. In sanctifying homosexual unions, we have committed National Apostasy #2. The name "Obergefell" means "O Mountain Fell" and even more interestingly, Hodges was the Director of the government's Health Department!

Not only are entire nations now "sanctifying perversions" but so are entire denominations. With each passing day, we see another news story of church compromise on the holiness and sanctity of marriage. We must, like Peter and John, present the irrefutable evidence. This evidence is the life-giving miracle of Holy Matrimony between one man and one woman which is a shadow-picture of Christ and His Bride.

Placing our life-giving body parts into a waste receptacle is not only physically damaging, but it brings national DEATH. Scripture tells us to "run from sexual sin" (1 Corinthian 6:18 NLT) just as Lot fled Sodom. No other sin has the potential to destroy the temple more quickly.

The evidence is clear. This argument is more than forty years old. Entire civilizations have failed because of this sin. No one can refute it anymore. One glance at a medical book or photos of a "gay" pride parade and we can see that this has crossed the Rubicon in terms of physical and societal disease.

This is why the opposition against those coming out of the homosexual lifestyle is so incredibly fierce. In California, people who have been healed of homosexuality wear a simple T-shirt with one message:

"CHANGED"

Let's present this same irrefutable evidence like Peter and John:

> Be it known unto you all, to all the people of Israel, that by the Name of Jesus Christ of Nazareth, whom ye crucified, whom God raised from the dead, even by him doth this man stand here before you whole.   ~ Acts 4:10 (KJV)

> And beholding the man which was healed standing with them, they could say nothing against it.   ~ Acts 4:14 (KJV)

When a healed person, formerly mentally and spiritually destroyed by sin disease, is standing before the Council for consideration, it is more evidence than can possibly be refuted. When the cry of "Born this way" is offered as an impediment to healing, we offer back this biblical example.

Like the lame man, we are all "born this way"...born into a fallen world of sin! However, we are able to be rescued, healed and changed by the Power of Jesus Christ. The evidence is irrefutable.

Let's be like Rahab and raise the red flag of alarm. Then, we must raise the white flag of surrender to God through REPENTANCE. We must, as a nation, completely get "over the rainbow" or our City on a Hill will vanish like a dream.

Until we REPENT of this serious sin, we will not get a national clean bill of health. Like Rahab, we need to begin placing our trust in God Almighty. For a starting point, let's each start with ourselves. When it comes to showing the world that the Power of Christ can really change us...there's no place like home.

4 NATIONAL APOSTASIES:

1) Innocent Slaughter
2) **Sanctification of Perversions**
3) Removal/Replacement of God Almighty in the public square and in the churches
4) Betrayal of the Throne of David

Repentance Prayer:

Heavenly Father, I REPENT for any times I failed to present Your irrefutable evidence. You told us in Your Holy Word that You made man and woman and the two shall become one flesh (Matthew 19:4-6 ESV) and we dare not pronounce any other false combinations that are a perversion of Your plan. Help me to proclaim the gospel through the healing Power of Jesus Christ. Teach me to show others, through the obvious and evident changes in my own life, the undeniable strength of Christ to heal and restore. We pray this prayer in the Name of Yeshua who is our Great Physician. ~ Amen

Scriptures to help me cleanse with His Word:

_____

_____

_____

Pastor Jeffrey Daly

DAY #39
Stuck in Neutral
Gag Reflex

40 and More Men Vowed not to Eat
or Drink until Paul Killed

*So because you are lukewarm--neither hot nor cold--I am about
to vomit you out of My mouth!*
Revelation 3:16 (Berean Study Bible)

Often it appears as if the devil's crowd seems to have more *passion* than the church! This has always bothered me. In today's "40/40's" found in scripture, we see there were more than forty men who vowed not to eat or drink anything until they killed Paul:

> *When daylight came, the Jews formed a conspiracy and bound
> themselves with an oath not to eat or drink until they had killed
> Paul. More than forty of them were involved in this plot.*
> ~ Acts 23:12-13 (Berean Study Bible, emphasis added)

I don't know about you, but this devotional study has given me a new and deep understanding of what "forty" really symbolizes in scripture. It's almost as if, in the spiritual world, once we reach the "forty" mark it's..."GAME ON!"

Among God's people, fasting should be a regular discipline. By now, we know that the stakes are high. Shouldn't we, at least, have more resolve than those who are obviously filled with evil?

Think of the evil passion that has brought us to this precarious tipping point today in our nations...the passion of feminists, the Pro-Death crowd, Leftists, Marxists, LGBTQ+ activists, and atheists.

I once heard a great Pro-Life speaker ask: "If we really believe abortion to be the horror that it is...Why are we not throwing our bodies across the doors of these death clinics?" Good question. Passion is what propels us into action.

We have passively sat by and allowed Bible reading and prayer to be removed from our children's education. We have passively allowed the sexual revolution to roll over us...perhaps we even participated. We have allowed millions of babies to be slaughtered on our watch and now we are seeing the medical perversion of our children, unlike anything in the history of mankind. The "progressive" steamroller continues to move "Forward" with an ever-increasing intensity of evil passion.

Today we come to the third National Apostasy that causes a nation to be destroyed. It is the removal and replacement of God Almighty in our public square. Now, it's very fashionable today to call on "God" as some undefined, squishy, "whatever you want Him to be" Spirit in the sky. I think this is even more prevalent in so-called democratic nations where we have been spoon-fed on the fanatical religion of "fairness."

So, how's this neutral public square working out for us?

There's a reason God says He vomits out the lukewarm. It's because He knows that, ultimately, there is no such thing as "middle ground." Even Hollywood plots and secular philosophers despise the guy who "plays the middle." Dante famously said:

The hottest places in hell are reserved for those who, in a period of moral crisis, maintain their neutrality.

"Religious Freedom" is an oxymoronic non-sequitur. There is NO freedom when we allow all demonic religions equal footing to co-rule our land. The devil creates bondage, not liberty. Think about it: Satanism is a "religion." Should we support Satanic rituals dictating public policy?

Let's take it down a notch. How about Islam? Should we, as a nation, encourage laws based on Sharia? Let's take it down a notch again. How about Hinduism. Do we want seven demons to rush into our neutral "swept-clean" public square? How about Buddhism? Surely, that is so "peaceful," right? Buddhism teaches that each human being is a "god" unto himself. Umm...wait a minute. Now we are getting somewhere. In fact, I think we have arrived! Human secularism *is* simply the worship of self. With the open sale of butchered baby parts over the Internet, perhaps we are getting an understanding of just how ugly this really is.

We were never instructed by God to allow "freedom of religion." We were instructed by Jesus Christ to teach strangers in our land in His Way and Truth based on Judeo-Christian Mosaic Law values. Then, they will begin to appreciate the God who is responsible for our peaceful and blessed nation.

> *And if a stranger dwells with you in your land, you shall not mistreat him. The stranger who dwells among you shall be to you as one born among you, and you shall love him as yourself: for you were strangers in the Land of Egypt: I am the Lord your God. Therefore, you shall observe <u>all</u> My statutes and <u>all</u> My judgments, and <u>perform them:</u> I am the Lord.*
> ~ Leviticus 19:33-34 & 37 (NKJV, emphasis added)

The term "stranger" means "stranger to the One True God." To "love him as yourself" means to help make strangers *un-estranged* from our Holy God! God is commanding us to introduce them to the God of the Old and New Testament. Leviticus 19 is the Old Testament equivalence to Jesus' Great Commission! We too, were once in "Egypt" (lost in our sins). We cannot follow God's command when our nation's public policy is nothingness or an impure mish-mash of demon-inspired religions.

Yet the folly from our pulpits and legislators continues with Christian leaders actually pushing for and satisfied with "religious freedom" laws that further neutralize our public square. We cannot run our country on any other foundation than a Judeo-Christian one. If we value liberty, anything else is sinking sand.

> *Now the Lord is that Spirit: and where the Spirit of the Lord*
> *is, there is Liberty.* ~ 2 Corinthians 3:17 (KJV)

"Hey, that's really narrow, Jesus. Perhaps You need to be a little more tolerant. You don't want to be called a hater, right Jesus? Maybe You should take a class in cultural diversity."

When we think we know more than Jesus Christ...there really is nothing more revolting. The scripture tells us that this attitude makes God want to projectile vomit.

If we don't stop swallowing this tasteless "neutral" garbage...

We may just get hurled.

4 NATIONAL APOSTASIES:

1) Innocent Slaughter
2) Sanctification of Perversions
3) **Removal/Replacement of God Almighty in the public square and in the churches**
4) Betrayal of the Throne of David

Repentance Prayer:

Heavenly Father, I REPENT for the times I failed to uphold Your command to love the strangers in our land as myself. If I know that You are the Spirit of Liberty, I am commanded by Your Holy Word, in both the Old and New Testament, to share this message with others. Help me to proclaim the gospel through the healing Power of Jesus

Christ. I turn away from my thoughts and my ways to the Only Way through the Blood of Jesus Christ. Let me not attempt to use false spiritual power that is of no use in Your Kingdom battle. Help me to GO and make disciples of all nations. Help us to REPENT and then lead others off the pathway of destruction. We pray this in the Name above all names, the King of kings, the Lord of lords, Jesus Christ/Yeshua our Lord and Savior. ~ Amen

Scriptures to help me cleanse with His Word:

_____

_____

_____

DAY #40
Game of Thrones
A King's Ransom

40 Stripes "Save One" was the Whipping Paul Endured

Then I saw thrones, and the people sitting on them had been given the authority to judge. And I saw the souls of those who had been beheaded for their testimony about Jesus and for proclaiming the Word of God. They had not worshiped the beast or his statue, nor accepted his mark on their forehead or their hands. They all came to life again, and they reigned with Christ for a thousand years. ~ Revelation 20:4 (NLT)

The fourth and Final National Apostasy is "Betrayal of the Throne of David." First, let me note that much of the Western World has already committed National Apostasies #1, #2 and #3. We would be hard pressed to find a Western "civilized" nation that doesn't permit abortion, sanction perversion and attempt to remove God Almighty from the public square.

Apostasy #4 is the equivalent of committing spiritual suicide. When we betray Israel, we betray the Throne of David. There is both a temporal *and* spiritual Israel that we must be conscious of. Even in their well-chronicled failings, the Israelites have been a light to us. We must love the Jewish people and be incredibly grateful that this people birthed the greatest Gift of all: Yeshua.

How do we specifically betray the Throne of David? Since Yeshua now sits on this Throne in the Heavenlies, any failure to proclaim His Name and

His Word is a betrayal. His Words did not begin in Matthew, no matter what "red-letter" churches may attempt to teach. Before He came in the flesh as a little child in a manger, He *was*, He *is* and He always *will be*. He walked with Adam and Eve in the garden, He showed up at Abraham's tent, He wrestled with Jacob, He announced the birth of Samson to Manaoh, He was in the furnace with Shadrach, Meschach and Obednego, and He spoke to Daniel at the Tigris River.

Thus, when the Heavenly Throne declares that Israel, through Abraham, will possess a certain parcel of land, He means forever. Any government that attempts to make a false "peace" deal with those who hate Israel, is marked for destruction. Curse Israel and you are, in essence, attempting to curse God. Job's wife said: *"Curse God and die."* ~ Job 2:9(b) (NKJV). That statement can be taken as horribly bad advice or simply read as an absolute fact. Curse God and you will die.

So whether it be a decree by the UN or an "artful deal," anyone that seduces Israel, temporal or spiritual, to disbelieve God's promises or act out of accordance with His promises, will be the equivalent of a spiritual Judas. Like Judas, any nation or nations who support this will have their inward parts spilled out in a field of blood.

By the Providence of God, we could not end this "40/40's" series with a more appropriate reference than Paul's *"forty stripes save one."*

Today, we take encouragement that Paul was spared that last, final stripe. Paul represents all of us. God gave us Saint Paul the Apostle so we can observe, by his example, the working out of our salvation through Christ in fear and trembling. His Holy Spirit-inspired Letters to the Church are much needed balm to prepare this "body of death" for the resurrection.

We, indeed, *deserve* that last stripe, but Jesus took it instead. His skin was flayed to save ours. In being set free from punishment, we gladly return to Him as willing bondservants. With God's vision of us as a sanctified Bride without spot or wrinkle, you and I are zealous to repent in order to "live up" to His high ideal!

What is mankind that God is mindful of us? Let us follow Paul's exhortation:

> +*As a prisoner in the Lord, then, I urge you to walk in a manner worthy of the calling you have received.*
> ~ Ephesians 4:1 (Berean Study Bible)

4 NATIONAL APOSTASIES:

1) Innocent Slaughter
2) Sanctification of Perversions
3) Removal/Replacement of God Almighty in the public square and in the churches
4) **Betrayal of the Throne of David**

Repentance Prayer:

Heavenly Father, I REPENT for the times I failed to support Israel temporally or spiritually. Help me not to commit spiritual suicide, but instead openly proclaim that Your Promises will always come to pass. We acknowledge that Your Hand is upon temporal and spiritual Israel and no one is able to wrest this parcel of tillage from your Holy grasp. Let us not support any false "peace" deals that attempt to divide what You have declared must not be divided. Help me to follow Your instructions to GO and make disciples of all nations. Help us to REPENT and then lead others off the pathway of destruction. We pray this in the Name above all names, the King of kings, the Lord of lords, Jesus Christ/Yeshua our Lord and Savior. ~ Amen

Scriptures to help me cleanse with His Word:

Humble Abode
Closing Prayer of Repentance

For I am jealous over you with a godly jealousy: for I have espoused you to One Husband that I may present you as a chaste virgin unto Christ. ~ 2 Corinthians 11:24 (KJV)

We conclude with a Holy Spirit-inspired prayer donated by one of our members. We pray that this Devotional series has increased your reverence for the Holiness and Sovereignty of God's Holy Word and has brought you into greater intimacy with Yeshua our Messiah.

Please feel free to share these Devotionals and Prayers and for further reflection.

As you go, preach this message: "The Kingdom of Heaven is near." Heal the sick, raise the dead, cleanse the lepers, drive out demons. Freely you have received; freely give.
~ Matthew 10:7-8 (Berean Study Bible)

Prayer of Repentance

Dear Heavenly Father: Thank you for Your unfailing love. Help us to love You fully in return and worship You in a spirit of Truth. We humbly ask now for open heavens. Let it rain Your Living Water to cleanse this world of all evil. As we enter a time of deep global darkness, we desperately need Your Light. Without You our righteousness is as filthy rags, but with You we can become upright through accepting and sharing the atonement You have procured for us on the Cross. Remind us that there can only be unity among those who declare You as their Father and not with children of the devil. Wherever we may find the True Church, those born again of the Holy Spirit, teach us to bear with one another in love, and maintain unity in the bond of peace. We look onward to Your soon return as our Bridegroom when we will be one with You forever. Let us avoid all unholy alliances and unequal yokes. Help us to walk straight, but more importantly, when we stumble, help us to walk true even when it doesn't seem like the logical path. Enable us to sow good seed and readily volunteer to be a laborer in Your harvest fields. Keep us humble as we wait with anticipation for Your next direction. Let us not envy others nor desire our own way. Enable us to temper our anger and avoid wrath as we remember our own weaknesses and Your merciful grace. Remind us to clothe ourselves in spiritual armor and in Your garments of righteousness so that we are prepared to fight and celebrate the victory with You. We thank You for all of our blessings and acknowledge You and You alone as our Master as we eschew the false idols of this world. Help us to get all of our satisfaction fully realized in our relationship with You. Command us to bring back a good report of faith and have the boldness to take the land. Teach us to obey Your commandments right away and all the way, with alacrity and eagerness. We recognize that it is time for another exodus from the evil systems of this world. Comfort us with the knowledge that Your Word is written all over our hearts and minds and it is a lamp unto our path. Restrain us from chaos and disorder and teach us to humbly walk in Your ways. It is a joy to think that, through faith, we can be included in Your Epic Drama to help release the captives of the world from the enemy's plan to steal, kill and destroy. We realize that You are looking for those of us who are willing to serve and also be prostrate before You. Though we face major obstacles and seeming giants, we know that You are the Champion of the underdog. Let us not shirk from our responsibility to speak out even if we are accused of having strong language. We understand that cowards will not overcome and are the very first to be refused entry into Your Kingdom. Allow our hearts to be burdened by the suffering we see around us and be ready to supply the balm of Gilead. Demonstrate to us that silence is not an option and we must speak out for those being led away to slaughter. Open our eyes as we obtain our eye salve from You. Empower us to develop a heart of discernment which exposes the worthless works of the enemy and false religious practices which have no ability to tear down enemy strongholds. Communicate the necessity for us to not proclaim victory in our own strategies, inventions and plans but to fully rely on You as our Leader. Prompt us to hand over all unclean and empty habits which have developed over years of practice. In times past, You have graciously overlooked our ignorance, but now You are calling us all to repent. May we offer ourselves wholly as a living sacrifice to do Your will. Let us offer up the sweet smell of the incense of a pure heart on Your altar. In our innermost being, prompt us to develop a strong desire to serve You with all our hearts, souls, minds and strength. As the time for Your arrival seems closer and closer, let us not fail to be watchmen on the wall proclaiming Your message of repentance even as we individually must repent and humble ourselves as well. Support us as we resist the devil and he flees from us in the Power of Your Holy Name. Put us back into alignment as You re-aligned the First Century Church after Your resurrection. We willingly hand in our ashes in return for Your unfathomable Beauty. Keep us from the powerful delusion and from the evil one as we resist the secularism of the world's false teachings and reaffirm Your plan for Your children to be fruitful and multiply. Remind us that there is no room in Your Kingdom for lukewarm service and that full devotion to You is a necessary requirement. As princes, kings, and kingdoms fall, we look upward for our salvation draws nigh. We pray this prayer in the Name above all names, the King of kings, the Lord of lords, our God and Savior, Jesus Christ of Nazareth, the Name under which every knee must bow and every tongue confess, that You, indeed, are Lord. ~ Amen

Acknowledgements

We honor Our Father and The Church, wherever she may be found.

The Marys, those who choose the better part, who love much, who pour out of their own substance, those who labour and whose souls magnify the Lord.

The Nathaniels, those without guile.

The Peters, those who confess the Rock of their Salvation.

The Disciples, those who have left house, wife, brothers, parents or children to follow Him.

The Centurions, those with great faith in the public square.

The Givers, especially those who give all they have.

The Penitents, those who confess their sins and ask for Mercy.

The Sick, those who reach out to touch His Garment.

The Thirsty, those who share Living Water from the well.

The Gentiles, those who are thankful for crumbs from the Master's Table.

The Flesh-diseased, those who remember to return and say "thank you."

The Innocents, the little children who are welcomed into the Kingdom.

The Preachers of Repentance, the greatest born of women.

The Friends, those whom He loves.

The Children of Israel. You are imprinted on the Palm of His Hands, never to be forgotten.

> Well done, thou good and faithful servants. Well done.

About The National
Day of Repentance

We are a growing group of believers in Jesus Christ/Yeshua, drawn by His Scripture and His Holy Spirit, to begin purifying ourselves as His Bride through the privilege of Repentance. The Father is calling for a culture of repentance in His Body. He wants us to turn our heads and hearts to follow Him.

What exactly is "The National Day of Repentance" and why is this so important to you personally? History and Biblical Scripture tells us that all nations with internal "moral decay" have eventually become fallen empires, no matter how large or how powerful. At NDR, we believe that many nations are sadly on this same pathway and that the "set time has come" (Psalm 102:13 NKJV). Unless we embrace, both personally and nationally, a true repentant attitude and return to our Judeo-Christian foundations, we will soon be ruled by tyranny. The Bible clearly states that the outcome of our current disobedience of innocent slaughter, sanctification of perversions, removal/replacement of the One True God from our public square and, ultimately, Betrayal of the Throne of David, will result in bondage and destruction.

Repentance and humility are key to entering the Kingdom of the Living God. Yeshua/Jesus' very first word as He began His Ministry was "REPENT." Once in the Kingdom, Repentance is also a vital process by which the Lord restores our soul and leads us in the path of His Righteousness for His Name's sake. Yeshua thus calls us to be ZEALOUS TO REPENT so as to overcome and sit with Him on His Throne (Revelation 3:19-21 NKJV). Repentance is especially key to healing those nations who were founded on Mosaic Law and wish to participate in the Covenant relationship.

When God has "shut up Heaven" or has "sent pestilence among my people," we need to remember His advice:

If My people, who are called by My Name, will humble themselves, and pray and seek My face, and turn from their wicked ways, then I will hear from Heaven, and will forgive their sin and heal their land.

~ 2 Chronicles 7:14 (NKJV)

As joint believers in the Most High God, we can take the example of Nehemiah who, prior to being anointed to rebuild the walls, confessed his own sins, the sins of his father's house, and his nation's sins. Having repented, he could later say that the joy of the Lord was his strength.

If you have never prayed to Jesus Christ the Messiah, we urge you to REPENT and do so now. He is faithful and will answer the prayers of the truly penitent. If you have already submitted your life to Christ the Savior, we ask you to come along side this ministry as a fellow prayer warrior. Then continue to pray as God leads you to entreat for Repentance in your family, your local community and your country.

There is no time to waste. The "enemy" is crouching at the door and seeking to devour us. Let's hold fast in unity, fasting, prayer and true heartfelt Repentance as we ask God for Mercy.

Joel 2: 12-14(a): (The Message)
But there's also this, it's not too late—
God's personal Message! –
"Come back to Me and really mean it!
Come fasting and weeping, sorry for your sins!"
Change your life, not just your clothes.
Come back to GOD, your God.
And here's why: God is kind and merciful.
He takes a deep breath, puts up with a lot,
This most patient God, extravagant in love,
Always ready to cancel catastrophe.
Who knows? Maybe He'll do it now,
Maybe He'll turn around and show pity.

About Pastor Jeffrey Daly
Founder & Director of The
National Day of Repentance

A former Wall Street lawyer, atheist and New-ager, Jeffrey was struck one day with a deep moment of spiritual insight from the Holy Spirit. In addition to clearly hearing God's call to *"Do My Work,"* he was filled with the knowledge of this particular scripture:

> *He who speaks from himself seeks his own glory, but He who seeks the glory of the One who sent Him is true, and no unrighteousness is in Him.* ~ John 7:18 (NASB)

It was then, in 1991, that he repented of the personal glory-seeking of the New Age movement and has committed his life to serving Christ ever since. He formerly pastored, along with his wife Laurie, the Jesus Christ Fellowship in Middletown, California. During his years of legal practice, he received The Pacific Institute's Faith & Justice Award for his defense of faith and family values. Recently retired from his legal practice, he now spends his time writing, teaching and working with other national repentance and prayer ministries. In addition to founding the National Day of Repentance, he is also a director of Capitol Hill Prayer Partners in Washington, DC.

His passion is to preach about the power and gift of repentance so that we, as His Bride, will be ready for the soon return of Jesus Christ/Yeshua the Messiah, our beloved Bridegroom. This Devotional is his fourth book on Repentance.

His other books are available at www.repentday.com

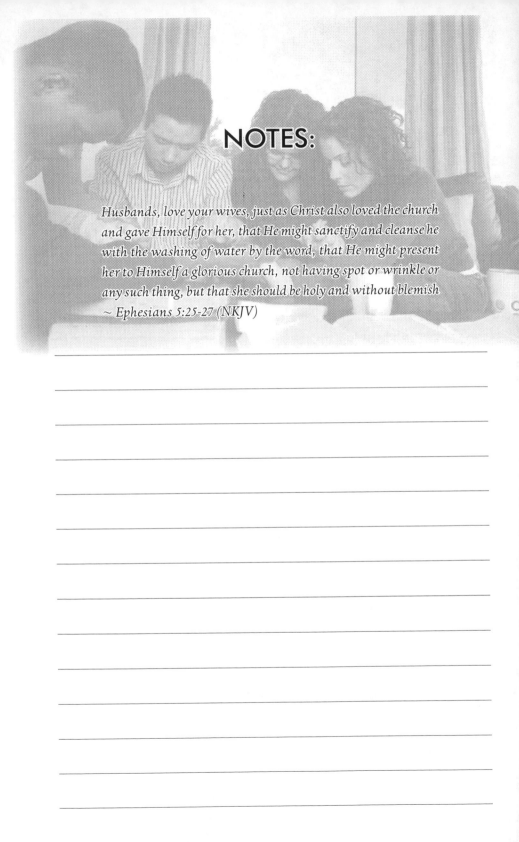

NOTES:

Husbands, love your wives, just as Christ also loved the church and gave Himself for her, that He might sanctify and cleanse he with the washing of water by the word, that He might present her to Himself a glorious church, not having spot or wrinkle or any such thing, but that she should be holy and without blemish
~ Ephesians 5:25-27 (NKJV)

NOTES:

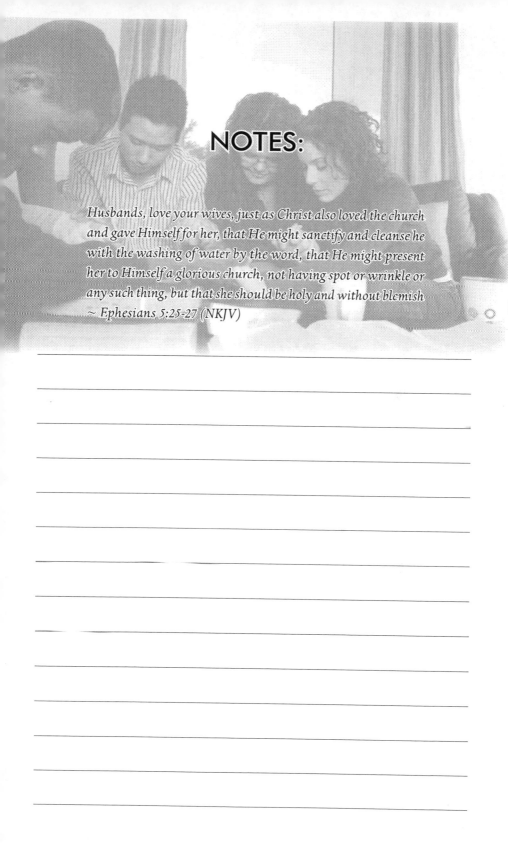

Husbands, love your wives, just as Christ also loved the church and gave Himself for her, that He might sanctify and cleanse he with the washing of water by the word, that He might present her to Himself a glorious church, not having spot or wrinkle or any such thing, but that she should be holy and without blemish ~ Ephesians 5:25-27 (NKJV)

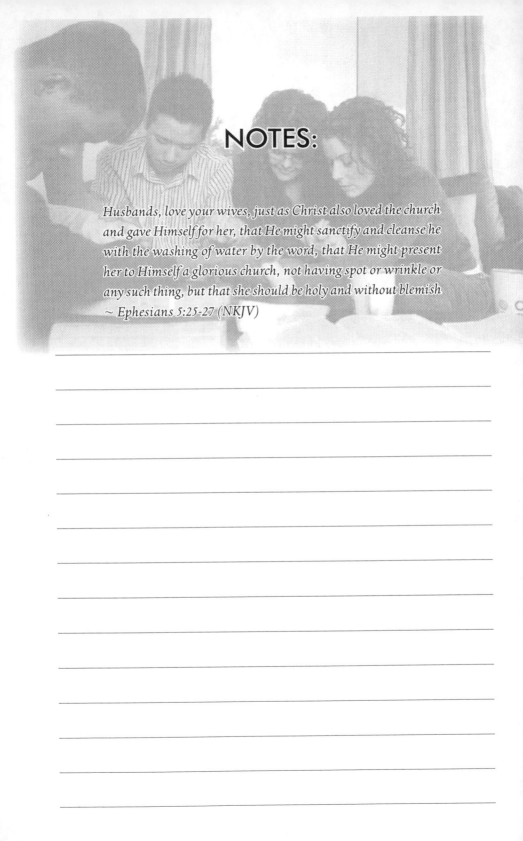

NOTES:

Husbands, love your wives, just as Christ also loved the church and gave Himself for her, that He might sanctify and cleanse he with the washing of water by the word, that He might present her to Himself a glorious church, not having spot or wrinkle or any such thing, but that she should be holy and without blemish
~ Ephesians 5:25-27 (NKJV)

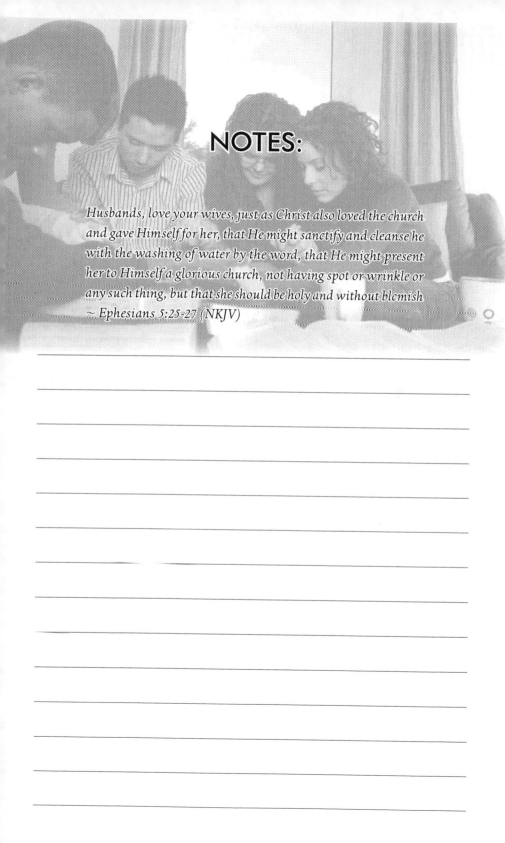

NOTES:

*Husbands, love your wives, just as Christ also loved the church
and gave Himself for her, that He might sanctify and cleanse her
with the washing of water by the word, that He might present
her to Himself a glorious church, not having spot or wrinkle or
any such thing, but that she should be holy and without blemish*
~ Ephesians 5:25-27 (NKJV)

Printed in the United States
By Bookmasters